Four Great Rivers to Cross

Four Great Rivers to Cross

Cheyenne History, Culture, and Traditions

Patrick M. Mendoza
Ann Strange Owl-Raben
Nico Strange Owl

1998

TEACHER IDEAS PRESS

A Division of

Libraries Unlimited, Inc.

Englewood, Colorado

TEACHER IDEAS PRESS
A Division of
Libraries Unlimited, Inc.
P.O. Box 6633
Englewood, CO 80155-6633
1-800-237-6124
www.lu.com/tip

Production Editor: Kay Mariea
Copy Editor: Jason Cook
Proofreader: Cherie Rayburn
Indexer: Susan Zernial
Interior Design and Layout: Judy Gay Matthews

Library of Congress Cataloging-in-Publication Data

Mendoza, Patrick M.
    Four great rivers to cross : Cheyenne history, culture, and
traditions / Patrick M. Mendoza, Ann Strange Owl-Raben, Nico
Strange Owl.
        x, 135 p.   22x28 cm.
    Includes bibliographical references and index.
    ISBN 1-56308-471-6
    1. Cheyenne Indians--Study and teaching (Elementary)   2. Cheyenne
Indians--Study and teaching (Middle school)   I. Strange Owl-Raben,
Ann.   II. Strange Owl, Nico.   III. Title.
E99.C53M45   1997
973'.04973'0071--dc21   97-30742
                                                              CIP

Contents

Contents *(continued)*

Acknowledgments

Deserving of special thanks are Grace Strange Owl, our beloved mother/grandmother, and Dayton Raben our husband/father, who took the time and had the foresight to record the family legends translated for this publication. Without their efforts made more than 30 years ago, we would not have been able to complete this project.

We would also like to thank Pat Mendoza for his encouragement and enthusiasm for this project, as well as our aunt/grandmother Sue Wilson for her help in translations. Also so vital are the efforts and long hours spent by Wayne Leman, Ted Risingsun, and Josephine Stands In Timber Glenmore in translating and compiling the contents of the Cheyenne dictionaries and linguistic audiocassettes, for these efforts help the Cheyenne people to stave off at least one of the catastrophic predictions of Sweet Medicine by helping us to learn and keep our language alive.

—Ann Strange Owl-Raben
Nico Strange Owl

Credits

Cover art by Albert Harjo (painting name: *The Last Goodbye*). Albert Harjo is a full-blood Creek.

Drawings on frontispieces of the Old Man and Young Woman by Ruth Cox.

Maps on pages 58, 84, and 85 by Cheryl Tongue.

Photographs on pages 63, 64, and 66 courtesy of Colorado Historical Society.

Photograph on page 77 courtesy of Castillo de San Marcus National Park.

Photographs on pages 130 and 131 by Lee Milne.

Grace and David Strange Owl in about 1960. Grace was the great-granddaughter of William Bent and Owl Woman.

Introduction

The purpose of this book is to help teachers weave their way through the complex culture of the people we call the Cheyenne Indians.

The word "Indian," of course, is not an accurate name for any of the native people who dwelled in this land. I recently saw a T-shirt that read, "In 1492, Christopher Columbus was discovered lost at sea by Native Americans." To me, that statement is more accurate than many of the statements presently taught in schools about Columbus. He was lost and named the native people of the island of San Salvador "Indians" because he thought he was in the Spice Islands near India. Since that time, there have been many stereotypes and myths created about Native American cultures.

This book was conceived with the idea of bringing into print an accurate account of the Tse Tse Stus (Tsétsėhéstahese), or Cheyenne, culture. There are many misconceptions about the Native Americans who have inhabited this land for thousands of years. All Native Americans do not pray alike, look alike, or believe in the same things. Many of these cultures have similarities, but each is unique. To say that their religions are the same would be like saying that Baptists and Catholics are the same because they are both Christian. To say that their languages are alike would be like saying that Spanish, French, Italian, and English are exactly alike because they are rooted in Latin. As a last example, the word *squaw*, commonly used in other books and movies, is a very derogatory term which implies an "old hag" or much worse. Please do not use this word when studying Native American culture.

This book contains a collection of stories, both historical and cultural. The narrative of this book takes place in a real setting but in the lives of the fictitious Old Nam Shim (Namėšéme), which means "grandfather," and a little girl named Shadow. The traditional tales, language, and stories of the ceremonies all come from my coauthors Ann Strange Owl-Raben and her daughter Nico Strange Owl. Fortunately, for all of us, Ann's husband, Dayton Raben, had written down many of these stories verbatim from Ann's mother and grandmother before they passed away. Ann's grandmother was 109 years old when she died.

The history of the Cheyenne came from many sources, including my Cheyenne brother, John Sipes Jr., who is the Southern Cheyenne tribal historian and the great-great-grandson of the woman warrior Mochi, mentioned in this book. One of the proudest days of my life was the day his family formally adopted me. Even before that time and since, I have been treated as family, not only by his family, but also by my wonderful coauthors. Since my first involvement with the Tse Tse Stus 11 years ago, many wonderful family stories have been shared with me.

The dialogue text in this book may sometimes not follow the rules of the "king's English" because the Cheyenne have their own way of using the English language.

Read this book from beginning to end, or you will miss the chronological sequences set forth in this story. Chapter one is requisite to understanding the narrative setting (Old Nam Shim and Shadow). It is an ideal reading supplement for any third- through eighth-grade student studying western history, Colorado history, Wyoming history, the Cheyenne wars, or anthropological studies of the Cheyenne culture.

The places mentioned in this book are located in Colorado, Montana, Wyoming, Nebraska, Kansas, Oklahoma, Texas, and South Dakota. Sample maps of several of these states are included on pages 58, 84, and 85.

Concluding each chapter of this book are student goals, activities, discussion questions, and bulletin board activities that can help students further understand and appreciate the stories in this book. At the end of the book is a vocabulary list of English and Cheyenne words and phrases used in the story, as well as some additional Cheyenne sayings that might interest students. A pronunciation guide for Cheyenne words is included with these vocabulary lists.

A note on Cheyenne spellings and pronunciations. The Cheyenne language was originally not a written language. English-speaking missionaries and academics eventually set the language into a written form. Depending on who you consult, there are naturally variations on the written forms. Compounding the issue is the fact that there are actually two dialects, Southern Cheyenne and Northern Cheyenne. Generally, throughout the text, we have used the Northern Cheyenne spellings. However, where Southern Cheyenne or family traditional spellings were more prominent in historical records, those spellings were used.

One last thought: Do not judge these stories because they are different from your own. Enjoy them and share them with someone who doesn't know anything about the culture. After all, this is what storytelling is about.

—Patrick M. Mendoza

1

Old Nam Shim

When he died, his face was a mass of wrinkles, a mass that could have easily been a map of the roads he traveled in the more than 105 years of his life. His work-torn hands lay folded across his chest, as his long, braided hair framed his arms and upper body. Gone from his dark brown eyes was the sparkle that had shown like a star in the night. Those eyes had seemed to be the compass point that guided his life on its journey. Old Nam Shim (Namẻšéme, grandfather) was dead, but his dreams and thoughts lingered on in those who knew and loved him—especially a 15-year-old girl the old man had called Shadow. He had called her Shadow because when the girl was young, she followed the old man everywhere—her parents had been killed in an automobile accident, and she was afraid to be left alone.

It was death that had brought together Shadow and Old Nam Shim, and now it was death that separated them. Her closest and only living relatives now were Old Nam Shim's grandson and his wife. They willingly took in the young girl, for in the old ways of the Cheyenne, no child was ever unwanted or unloved.

During this time of sadness and grief after her parents' death, her young mind tried to understand death. Why had death taken her mother and father? And what happened when one died? Were you just dead, or did your spirit continue to live? Was there such a thing as a spirit (séoto), and was that the same thing as a ghost? Shadow's young mind desperately sought to understand, for she had been caught between the influences of two civilizations: her own proud but waning people—the Tse Tse Stus (Tsétsẻhésta-hese), commonly called the Cheyenne—and the whites, who taught school and held church services at Lame Deer, on the Northern Cheyenne Reservation in Montana. It was Old Nam Shim who began to end her confusion about death and life by teaching Shadow the lessons she would one day need to know. It was he who entrusted Shadow with a great responsibility—his funeral. And it was he, in the years before his death, who taught Shadow the ancient ways and beliefs of the Cheyenne people.

Old Nam Shim comforted Shadow shortly after her parents' death by telling her that the Tse Tse Stus did believe in ghosts, and that ghosts were not to be feared. He said that shortly after a person dies, they often visit their loved ones in spirit form to say a final good-bye, or to tell of unfinished business. Old Nam Shim said that if Shadow should ever see a ghost, she should never turn her back to it. She should pay attention because this ghost would be trying to tell her something—to get something across. Old Nam Shim then promised Shadow that after he died, his ghost would return to let Shadow know that everything was all right.

Shadow remembered this lesson well, and as time passed, her trust in the old man and her natural curiosity took her on a wondrous journey through Nam Shim's mind. It was a journey that lasted 10 years. Now, Shadow would need all the knowledge Old Nam Shim had shared with her to help him complete his final journey. Old Nam Shim would have to cross the Four Great Rivers to reach the passageway to Seyon (Séáno), the Place of the Dead, beyond the route of the Milky Way. Before her grandfather could complete this journey, Shadow would need to accomplish many things.

First, Shadow had to notify the old "spiritual man" with whom Nam Shim had become very close. After his arrival at Old Nam Shim's home, this friend said a prayer while purifying the house and purifying the body of Old Nam Shim. He then painted Old Nam Shim's body with mineral paints. This ritual signified that Old Nam Shim had lived his full circle of life. The few items of the material world Old Nam Shim favored were placed into his pine coffin. His body was dressed in jeans, a new ribbon shirt, and beaded moccasins that Shadow and Nam Shim's granddaughter had made him for his journey through the Milky Way.

Shadow and other family members then placed Old Nam Shim's belongings outside his house for Old Nam Shim's friends and relatives to take. These same people would later bring new items to replace things they took. It was the Cheyenne way for the deceased's family to receive gifts. Many believe that this very complex network of giving and receiving has existed for centuries to help keep the tribe together.

Another of Shadow's duties was to notify the village crier. The crier announced Nam Shim's death by walking through the village, singing songs about him, and reminiscing about how Nam Shim had lived his life. He told the people that only two grandchildren, many great- and great-great-grandchildren, nieces and nephews, and Shadow survived him. The crier then told of the upcoming burial, feast, and giveaway. While this was happening, Shadow prepared a place for Old Nam Shim's burial.

The people from the white church and the BIA (Bureau of Indian Affairs) wanted Old Nam Shim buried in the white way, below the ground. "It is 1955," they told the Cheyenne elders and tribal leaders. "It is time the Cheyenne came into the twentieth century and gave up their old pagan ways." Shadow, though, had other ideas. She knew her people would help her by not saying a word about her plan to "bury" Old Nam Shim. Besides, the missionaries and the BIA people never watched the actual burial. How would they know what was done? It was Old Nam Shim's wish to be "buried" in the old traditional Cheyenne way—he wanted to be placed on a scaffold in a cottonwood tree.

The night before the burial, the traditional overnight wake was held in Old Nam Shim's home. The people, especially the women, grieved openly and wailed loudly. Food prepared by the family continued to cook in Nam Shim's kitchen. Tradition called for all the mourners to be well fed. During this time other family members and friends propped up Old Nam Shim's body in his coffin so that those who had known him could either embrace him or shake his hand. (The Cheyenne hold no fear of the deceased's body.) The wake lasted until morning's early hours, and by the time the last of the mourners had departed, Old Nam Shim's coffin had been filled with cards, gifts, and photos of family and loved ones. Nam Shim would take these things with him on his upcoming journey.

It was now time for Shadow and Old Nam Shim's grandson to fulfill their promise to him. With the help of a few uncles, cousins, and friends, they moved his coffin and all it contained to the place where the white man's "services" were held. The white missionaries, who had tried to convert Old Nam Shim for years, without success, wanted the funeral service to be held in a church. Shadow and the others agreed since this would be a show of "good faith" and would satisfy the missionaries. The Cheyenne people knew that the church people meant well and wanted to eulogize Old Nam Shim in their own way. They also knew that, for the missionaries, a funeral service was another chance to preach to the people. So, to make a good show for them, Old Nam Shim's grandson and his friends dug a grave for the onlooking whites, while family and friends stood in silence. Shadow knew that the church people would leave once they had finished preaching. Then the real ceremony could begin, in the traditional Cheyenne way, and the people could openly display their feelings without the intrusion of those who were trying to change their Cheyenne culture. This would also give Shadow, the grandchildren, and friends their chance to secret Old Nam Shim's body away after the missionary funeral.

When the missionaries had gone, Shadow and the others took Old Nam Shim's body and proceeded to a large cottonwood tree in the hills beyond Birney. Shadow and Nam Shim's grandson had already constructed a scaffold in the tree's great branches. Old Nam Shim himself had picked this tree and the particular branches that would hold the scaffold. Shadow remembered how the old man had said, "The branches remind me of two large arms. It would be nice to have them cradle my old body."

As the procession made its way up the hill, Shadow remembered all the wonderful times she had shared with this old man. Though Old Nam Shim lived a poor life in terms of the material world of the white man, he was for Shadow the richest of those who lived in hope, nonprejudice, and love. He met life as it came, the heartbreaks with the joys, always with a sparkle in his eyes. He was a pipe carrier and sun dancer—one who devoted his whole life to the protection and well-being of his people, the Tse Tse Stus.

She had learned from the stories the elders told, as well as from Old Nam Shim himself, that he was born sometime during the month of the Hard-Face Moon (He'konéneése'he, or November) in 1850, in the land of the Yellowstone (present-day Wyoming). His humble beginnings in a Tse Tse Stus birthing lodge, though, would soon be overshadowed. His exploits as a warrior were remembered by his own people, but not by the ve hoes (vé'ho'e, white men), who left behind the written words about the great wars.

Through the years, Shadow had learned of Old Nam Shim's early life from the other elders on the reservation. They were the ones who told her of how Old Nam Shim became a warrior at the age of 15, after his family was killed at a place the whites called Sand Creek (Póéneõ ó'he'e). On that cold November day of 1864, Old Nam Shim, together with hundreds of others who survived the slaughter, fled into the frozen sand hills in southeastern Colorado for protection from the white soldiers' murderous bullets.

From that day on, Nam Shim's adventures would take him from Colorado to Nebraska and Wyoming; then to Kansas, Oklahoma, and Texas; back to Oklahoma; and then on an incredible 1,500-mile journey to Montana, to a place called Little Big Horn. From there he was moved back to Oklahoma to a reservation, but in 1878 he would be a part of those Cheyenne who would again break away to go back to Montana and survive that terrible winter at Fort Robinson, Nebraska. It was during this time that a soldier shot him in his leg, causing him to limp for the rest of his life.

Shadow often wondered where Old Nam Shim had received his great wisdom. Had it been culled from all these places he'd been, or was it simply an endless beauty inside his heart? She didn't know, but she seemed to hear his voice again, as clearly as she had when he was alive, reminding her: "All I know is from what I've done in life—some good, some bad. I could tell you how I think things should be, but that isn't what life really is. It is different for each of us. Everything around us is alive, and we are related to all living things. And we can learn from all that's around us. See that big cottonwood tree by the river? Its branches dance in the wind, reaching out to what is felt but not seen, but the tree is held steady in the ground by its roots. If the branches bend too far, they will either break or uproot the tree. Just like that tree, you must be flexible, explore, and learn, but do not stray too far from your roots, our traditional ways. This way you will see many seasons, and the inner peace that life offers will grow inside you."

Old Nam Shim told stories to illustrate all the lessons of life he taught Shadow, stories that had been passed down through the generations, and stories that he had made up: "Little One, you and I are a lot alike, and yet so different. We are living proof of the circle in life. Your life is just beginning as my life nears its end. We both depend on my grandson and his wife to feed us and to nurse us through our times of sickness and need—me, because I'm getting too old to care for myself; you, because you are still too young. Your mind is searching through the clouds of 'whys' and 'whens' while my mind is often fogged because I'm getting too old to remember. What knowledge dawns in your mind becomes a fading shadow in mine."

Shadow also remembered the little things Old Nam Shim had done to tease her, like the time when they first talked. He was sitting on the banks of the Tongue River watching the sun go down. Shadow was only five at the time, and she asked Old Nam Shim what caused the sun's reflection on the water. Nam Shim smiled at her and, pointing to the sparkling river, said, "Little One, those are the water spirits lighting their torches for their night journey."

Shadow believed him. She found wonder and comfort in Nam Shim's stories and often recounted this one for others whenever she noticed water sparkle, telling them about the "spirits of the water." Shadow still believes Old Nam Shim's story, if only because it makes her feel good, and feel close to him, whenever she sees the sunlight on the water or feels the evening breeze on her face.

In this, her final journey with Nam Shim, Shadow let her mind go back to the stories he had told her of the earliest times of the Tse Tse Stus. These times were when more than just a trickle of water flowed down the bed of Big Sandy Creek (otherwise called Sand Creek) and the buffalo herds were so vast that it took days for all of them to cross one given point on the plains. He told her of when the cottonwood and juniper trees sang Summer's song of essence. Filled with life, Summer sang a chorus echoed by the rugged beauty of a land perfumed with sage, its melody orchestrated by miles of waving prairie and sweet grass. He told her stories of the changing seasons and reminded her of where to hunt sweetgrass, turnips, and other bounty that the seasons offered the people. He told Shadow of those times when their people roamed this land without sighting a white man. And he told her of the time their people were given the name Cheyenne from a Lakota word.

In the days of Nam Shim's grandfather's grandfather, before the Tse Tse Stus possessed horses, so the stories said, their people lived farther north, near a great lake and, later, near a vast river they called Missouri (an Algonguin word meaning "People of the Big Canoes"). When the white man's expansion forced the Tse Tse Stus to make their exodus from this land, they met another people called Lakota. These are the people whites call the Sioux. Because neither people understood the language of the other, the Tse Tse Stus were called Shaiheela, or Shai ena, which in Lakota means "people speaking a strange tongue." Later, when the French fur traders came into the villages, they heard the Lakota refer to the Tse Tse Stus as Shai ena. The trappers thought they had heard the French word *chien,* which means "dog." Since that time, other tribes, and eventually the white man, adopted the words Shai ena, or Cheyenne, for the Tse Tse Stus.

As a young boy, Nam Shim and other Cheyenne children often sat around the crackling warmth of village campfires and listened intently to old men talk about their tribe's traditions and lore, how they called themselves Tse Tse Stus, which in the Algonguin language means "people alike" or "our people." Often the young ones would have to bribe the old people with things like chokecherry pudding to tell them stories. The old ones told those young, wide-eyed listeners that the Tse Tse Stus once lived during a time of peace. It was a time before the horse, when the people stayed in one place, when men hunted on foot, and when it was the dogs that helped to carry supplies. During this time, people from all tribes, with different traditions and languages, lived in happiness and peace. With the coming of the horse, though, life changed for the Tse Tse Stus. This animal became the most sought-after possession on the Great Plains. Use of the horse gave the Tse Tse Stus, and other tribes, a mobility they had never before experienced. In fact, the Tse Tse Stus, like most Plains Indians, became superb horsemen. The horse made life easier for the Tse Tse Stus, but with its arrival came warfare.

Warfare to the Tse Tse Stus and other Indian tribes was not the brutal slaughter of an entire enemy. Great losses of life were rare in tribal fighting. Sporadic incidents of chance meetings, or a planned raid designed to quench revenge's thirst, constituted a great battle to the Plains Indians. Most importantly, war to the Tse Tse Stus was the love of combat, the honor and ritual it involved. The coming of the white man, though, taught the Tse Tse Stus the lessons of wholesale slaughter and the brutality of the white man's type of warfare.

In growing up, Old Nam Shim remembered how he and the other boys were taught the fundamental skills of being warriors and hunters. He told Shadow that he could still feel his muscles cramping from the hours he stood absolutely motionless while stalking game or an enemy. Stealth and cunning were instilled in males at an early age. With few exceptions, all became warriors. Yet Nam Shim and the other Tse Tse Stus were taught that counting coup in battle signified the most valiant warriors.

Counting coup involved a warrior riding up to an enemy brave and striking him with a lance or stick without killing him. Telling his stories to Shadow brought back the chase's pure exhilaration to Nam Shim; the fight's excitement stirred the fires of his mind as he recalled charging an armed enemy and escaping with life and limb intact. He remembered other legendary accounts of counting coup. Once, in a fight with some Pawnee, nine Tse Tse Stus counted coup on one warrior. The Pawnee left the battle alive, though bruised, battered, and sore.

Nam Shim became mythic for his many acts of not killing anyone. Taking a life held no honor for him. As a member of the Bow String Society, a warrior's society, Nam Shim's special talent, like old chief Yellow Wolf's, lay in stealing enemy horses. That talent helped make Yellow Wolf a chief. Old Big Foot, another member of the Bow String Society, was also noted for his ability to steal horses. The Tse Tse Stus told stories of how Big Foot once used a lasso to pull a fleeing Ute from his horse, claiming yet another four-legged prize.

Nam Shim told Shadow how young warriors learned the arts of hunting and warfare from the leaders of the warrior societies, but it was the old ones who enlightened all Tse Tse Stus about their creation. It was the same story Nam Shim told Shadow one summer night when they sat out in front of a campfire, though the "camp" was just outside his home. Old Nam Shim was too old to camp out again.

Discussion and Activities

Goals

■ Describe the customs followed by the Cheyenne people, and compare and contrast them with the customs followed by the white man.

■ Tell the story of how the Cheyenne people got their name.

■ Describe the relationship between the young and old in the Cheyenne culture and how it differs from the relationship in our own culture.

Discussion Questions

1. What are the most obvious differences between a Cheyenne funeral and the white man's funeral?

   Answer: The Cheyenne "buried" their dead on a scaffold either in a tree or in a high mound. White people bury their dead below the ground.

2. Why do you think the white men insisted Nam Shim's body be buried according to their customs? How did Nam Shim's family handle the situation? Do you think this was the best way they could have handled it? Explain.

   Answer: Will vary.

3. What are some of the other customs followed by the Cheyenne when someone dies?

   Answer: The possessions of the deceased are set out so that people of the tribe may take something to remember the deceased. In turn, these people bring gifts and food to the family of the deceased.

4. What does Nam Shim mean?

   Answer: Grandfather.

5. The telling of stories had brought Nam Shim and Shadow very close together. What was the purpose of these stories?

   Answer: To comfort Shadow in her grief for her parents and to teach her the ways of the Cheyenne culture.

6. What does Tse Tse Stus mean? How did the name Cheyenne come about?

   Answer: "Our people" or "people alike." Cheyenne was a name the Lakota (Sioux) gave to the Tse Tse Stus people. The name is derived from the Lakota words *Shai ena*, meaning "people who speak a strange tongue."

7. What is Seyon?

   Answer: The Place of the Dead.

8. After death, what must the Cheyenne cross to get to Seyon?

   Answer: The Four Great Rivers.

9. Where is Seyon?

   Answer: In the sky beyond the Milky Way.

10. What or who are the "water spirits"?

> ***Answer:*** The sun's reflection on the water at sunset.

11. What was Nam Shim's specialty in war?

> ***Answer:*** Stealing horses.

12. What was involved in counting coup? Why was it so important?

> ***Answer:*** It involved a warrior riding up to an enemy brave and sticking him with a lance or stick without killing him. Taking a life held no honor in and of itself. Counting coup or stealing horses was far more humiliating for the enemy because one had been able to outwit him.

Things to Do

Game of Tag—"Counting Coup"

The Cheyenne warriors counted coup, in which the object was not to kill your opponent, but to humiliate him by tagging him on the battlefield and then leaving him. This can be simulated with students through a game of tag. Divide the class into two equal groups and give each student three or four paper balls (crumpled up scrap paper). Have students throw the paper at each other while a student or two from each side tries to count coup on a member of the opposing side by tagging them. If they are hit with the paper, they are out of the game (it counts as a "kill"). If they are successful at tagging the member, they have successfully counted coup. Outside is the best location for this game, or in a gym.

Writing Activity

Counting coup is far different than the concept of war in the white man's culture. Ask your students the following questions:

- What do you think the white man thought of the practice of counting coup?

- Do you think this is a good way to conduct a war?

- Can you think of other ways in which differences could be settled without bloodshed?

Have students write a short story about settling differences in a manner that would be unique and not cause bloodshed.

Interviewing a Family Member

Shadow has a very special relationship with Nam Shim. He is passing down a knowledge of customs and culture to her through the stories he tells her. Have your students talk to or interview one of their grandparents, or another older family member, and ask them to tell a story of something that happened when they were younger. It might be a personal story about their life, a custom followed by the family, or a special person they remember. Have students practice telling their stories aloud, then have students tell the stories to the class. This activity allows students to experience oral storytelling and the passing on of a family story or tradition.

Family Histories

Oral stories were once the only way family histories were remembered and passed from generation to generation. Brainstorm with the class other ways we learn about our family histories today (e.g., photos, home movies, letters, scrapbooks, etc.). Have students document their family histories through modern means. Suggestions: collages of photos, timelines with drawings, or videotaped home movies.

Class Bulletin Board

As students learn about the Cheyenne culture, have them make charts, posters, maps, and illustrations of things they learn. Create a bulletin board or display area in the classroom where their work can be displayed. From this chapter, students could illustrate practices of Cheyenne warriors, make a chart to compare and contrast burial practices of the Cheyenne and the white man, and so on.

Library Research

In discussing the burial practices of the Cheyenne, students may become interested in investigating burial practices in other cultures. These burial practices often tell us a great deal about the religions of the culture, particularly their beliefs about an afterlife. Some interesting cultures to examine: ancient Egyptian, Indian (India), Native American (other than the Cheyenne). Once students have read about other cultures, they may want to present their information to the class. Make a chart of their findings and examine the similarities and differences among the cultures with the class.

2

Stories of Cheyenne Beliefs

The Cheyenne Creation Story

Shadow remembered how Old Nam Shim began his story. She remembered how the two of them stared at the fire's dancing flames as he began:

Shadow, a long time ago there was nothing in the great void we call the universe except the Creator, the one we call Maheo (Ma'heõ'o). He has always been there, and he created all that you see around you on the earth and in the heavens. It has been told in the Tse Tse Stus way that water once covered the earth. There were fish and birds but no animals. All of the birds Maheo created were water birds, but they had no place to nest. Maheo realized this and decided there must be a place for them to rest other than the water. So, He commanded a great warrior to fall from the sky into the water, and commanded him to find the earth's land. As the warrior floated on the surface, he beckoned all the waterfowl to him and told them to dive beneath the waters to search for mother earth. The swans, loons, and geese tried many times, but each failed. Then a little duck appeared. He took a deep breath and vanished deep into the water. He did not return for a long time, and the great warrior decided that surely the duck must have drowned. All of a sudden, he heard the noise of something surfacing in the water. He turned and saw the duck appear above the water's surface with what appeared to be mud on its bill. This small waterfowl had found earth where the geese, loons, and swans had all failed.

After the mud had dried, the breaths of the Four Great Grandfathers, the four winds, swept the dust away. As the dust touched the water, it thickened and grew and spread to create the landforms we now call earth's continents. And from that soft earth, something else was created: man and woman. They were called Summer and Winter because they are the two main

seasons. Isn't the early part of Fall much like the Summer, and the latter part more like the Winter? And isn't the early Spring like the Winter, and the latter part of that season like the Summer? The struggles of Summer and Winter on earth produced other climatic and seasonal changes. The sun is their joy, the rain their sorrow, and the icy winds and terrible summer storms their anger. These are the stories that have been told since our beginning.

And of our deities, the Tse Tse Stus call the great spirit of the sky The Wise One Above (He'ámávé'ho'e). Below earth, there lived another benevolent spirit, whom his people named The Wise One Below (Ahtó nové'ho'e). He possessed powers similar to The Wise One Above. And in the winds of the earth, there were four powerful spirits who dwelled at the four points of the compass.

To pay homage to these spirits, the ancient Tse Tse Stus created a ceremonial pipe made from red stone. This pipe is often called a "peace pipe," but it is used in all ceremonies we hold sacred, and in smoking, we always offer puffs of smoke to these six deities: first to the sky and earth, then to the winds of the east, south, west, and north. The Wise One Above is the chief god and creator, and in pipe ceremonies, the Tse Tse Stus always offered the stem to him before all others. Then they offered it to earth's great power. Since the beginning, we have implored The Wise One Below to make everything grow, so food might be bountiful and all might live. We pray to him, so the rivers and waters will flow, so all might drink and not suffer from thirst. And we pray to him, so the grass will grow, for the animals need nourishment from the land. Then we pray again, so the plants and herbs of medicine will flourish, so our people might heal themselves when ill.

After reverently offering the pipe to these great spirits, we offer its stem to the four directions, praying to the spirits who dwell there to calm the winds so our lodges will stay firmly on the ground. The east wind is always offered the first smoke, for all life arises from the land where the sun comes out of the ground. Then the pipe is offered to the south wind, for it is from this land where the warm winds are born. The pipe is then offered to the west wind, for all of life rests in the land where the sun goes back into the earth. Lastly, but never irreverently, the smoke is offered to the north wind, for it is in this land where the Winter dwells. For in this land of the Great Plains, the winds

Stories of Cheyenne Beliefs

blow more fiercely than anywhere else in North America, with the exception of the ocean shores. At times, Shadow, winds here equal a hurricane's ferocity. We Tse Tse Stus believe fervently in these spirits because many times, within minutes, we have seen days of perfect calm, with infinite visibility, change into days of blinding walls of rain or snow. We have also seen great changes of temperature brought on by the wind, when warm, summer-like days turned to freezing cold without warning. Shadow, I have always felt it wise to pray to all the gods, in one's own way. In our old ways, before the white missionaries, none of our people criticized another for their fervency in faith, or their lack of it. Religion has always been personal for the Tse Tse Stus.

The Time the Creator Came to Earth

Little One, when I was young, like you, the old ones told other stories to me and the other children. One of the stories I like most told of the arrival of The Wise One Above on earth and how he lived amongst the Tse Tse Stus.

The old man's memory drifted back to those days of youth, and he smiled at his thoughts.

Shadow, I have often thought of how wonderful it would have been to have lived in those days when The Wise One Above taught his people how to make spearheads from stone. From bone and stone, The Wise One Above taught the ancient Tse Tse Stus how to make knives for cutting meat and skin. What an honor it would have been to be the first of his people to be taught how to make bows and arrows by this great spirit. The Wise One Above also taught the Tse Tse Stus that buffalo, elk, deer, and earth's other animals were to be hunted for food and clothing. He taught the Tse Tse Stus to pray over those animals and thank them for their sacrifice.

I can only imagine the excitement of these ancient people when The Wise One Above taught them fire's secret. He informed the Tse Tse Stus that rubbing two sticks together at great speed created heat. The heat's acceleration then created a small flame. And he shared the secret of the two special stones, which, when swiftly struck together, caused sparks. He taught them about fire's benefit, so they might cook their food and stay warm during cold nights.

Sometimes, Shadow, I feel myself a little touched in the head when I think of these things. Still, I have wondered if all men dreamed of being alive when gods roamed the earth, of hearing their words, and of learning from them.

What do you think The Wise One Above's voice sounded like when he told the Tse Tse Stus that they were not alone in this world, that he had created other people, different from them, whom they would one day meet? And what did they feel when they learned that The Wise One Above had given these people the same gifts of fire, arrows, and knives? And we can only guess how The Great Wise One Above instructed the Tse Tse Stus to plant, grow, and cultivate corn from the earth.

During Old Nam Shim's final journey to his body's resting place, Shadow thought about these times and places. But her people's reality, since the time of Nam Shim's birth and before, revolved around the thousands of white men who had come to their land. Some of these white men were good, but many others disdained Shadow's people and customs. Their disdain for the Tse Tse Stus religion and land had been obvious. When she found herself getting angry at all white men because of what had happened to the Cheyenne—the reservation, poverty, and alcoholism—again Nam Shim's words came to her:

"Shadow, all people are the same: Indian, white, black—it makes no difference. I look at the deeds of a person, not the color. Color doesn't mean a thing. If we were all the same color and everyone was exactly the same, do you think that would end prejudice? True, no group of one color could hurt another group because we would all be the same color, but hate has far-reaching roots—if it doesn't find color, it will find something else. It always has. Color, religion, and beliefs have always been targets of hate. Bigotry is blind; it tries to destroy what it cannot see. Remember what I have said, and remember the prophecies of the one we call Sweet Medicine."

"Who was Sweet Medicine, Nam Shim?" asked Shadow.

Sweet Medicine

Long ago, Shadow, in the years of my father's grandfather's grandfather, tribal elders told stories about the prophet Sweet Medicine, how he came amongst the Tse Tse Stus before they owned horses. No one knew from where he came. They said an old Tse Tse Stus woman was gathering wood, and she heard a baby cry. She followed the sound to a hollow stump, where she found a beautiful baby boy. Not seeing anyone else around, the old woman called out for the parents, but no one answered. She decided to take the child home to her lodge that evening, hoping that the parents of the baby would come looking for him. When the people in the village learned that this old woman had a baby in her lodge, they all visited her to find out from where the child had come. The old woman told them how she had found the child, and that she did not know where his parents were.

The old woman raised the boy and named him Sweet Medicine. The other people who came to visit noticed that he was growing more quickly than other children. It was an amazing sight, and the people came

often to the old woman's lodge, just to watch Sweet Medicine. The Tse Tse Stus realized that this child was special. Sweet Medicine started walking and talking before any of the other children his age, and it was obvious to all that he possessed special powers. As a young child, Sweet Medicine would help the old woman he called "grandmother" by hunting for food or simply creating it from thin air.

As Sweet Medicine grew from an infant into a young man, which took only a few years, he showed great powers. When the tribe was hungry, he would lead the hunting parties to great herds of buffalo when no other could find them. It became known that Sweet Medicine was a wise and powerful medicine man who had visions of the future.

It is said that Sweet Medicine never married. During his time with the Tse Tse Stus, he demonstrated his great powers by helping our people form our government, and he made many predictions about the future of our people and the world. It is said that one day the Creator Himself came down to the most sacred of places, The Sacred Mountain (Nóvávóse)—what we call today Bear Butte, in South Dakota—and visited with Sweet Medicine in a cave. It was there that he gave Sweet Medicine the Sacred Medicine Arrows, and which Sweet Medicine in turn gave to the Tse Tse Stus. The Sacred Medicine Arrows are the Creator's channel for blessing and giving our people power to continue, for us, the animals and the plants of the earth to have food. When Sweet Medicine emerged from the cave on the Sacred Mountain, he carried a small basket of corn. He offered the corn to the hundreds of Cheyenne who had waited for him to return. This basket of corn was bottomless, and all the people ate until they were full. After the feast, Sweet Medicine gave the people the Sacred Medicine Arrows and gave them the rules by which they were to govern themselves. He told the Tse Tse Stus never to kill or lie, to respect women and children and never abuse them in any way. He then helped organize the Tse Tse Stus into bands and into the four societies that still govern the tribe to this day. He helped choose leaders and make our laws and policies.

Little One, when we talk of Sweet Medicine, it is always with reverence and awe. He told the Cheyenne of things that would happen in the future—things that have since come true—but things our people of years ago could not understand or visualize.

Our word for "white man" is ve hoe. The meaning of this word literally is "spider." We use this word because of one of Sweet Medicine's predictions. He told the Tse Tse Stus of long ago that a people with white skin would come to our land, and that they would be "wrapped" in something like a spiderweb. We now know that what he saw them wrapped in were clothes of woven wool and cotton cloth, much like the fine web of a spider. Many of Sweet Medicine's predictions have to do with the ve hoe. He told of many great things that these people would do, and of the destruction they would bring.

"There is a time coming," Sweet Medicine said, "when many things will change. Strangers will appear among you. Their skin will be light-colored, and their ways powerful. Their hair will be cut short, and they will speak no Indian tongue. Follow nothing these men do, but keep the ways that I have taught you, your own ways, as long as you can.

"One day the buffalo will disappear, but another animal will take its place. It will be an animal like the buffalo, but its hide will be slick. It will have a long tail and split hoofs, and you will learn to eat its flesh. Before this, though, there will be another animal, which you must learn to use. It will have a long, shaggy neck and a tail almost touching the ground. Its hoofs will be round. This animal will carry you on his back and help you in many ways. Those far hills in the distance take many days to reach now, but with this animal you will arrive there in a short time, so fear him not."

Then he told the people how the ve hoe would be able to travel from "blue ridge to blue ridge" in less than one day's time. He described what we now call the automobile. In another vision, he saw the ve hoe flying. The Tse Tse Stus thought that the ve hoe would be able to transform into birds and fly, but this is not what Sweet Medicine meant. He was describing things that we did not have words for at the time. He also saw airplanes flying across the water and great expanses of land. Sweet Medicine also told of a time when these people would leave the earth and find another place to live.

"Leave the earth?" a startled Shadow asked. "Nam Shim, do you think that's possible? I've seen movies about space travel, but do you think it's really possible?"

Little One, in my lifetime I have seen this earth when there were no cars, let alone airplanes, and my circle of life is still not complete. Of course I think it's possible, for I believe Sweet Medicine's prophecies. I've seen too many come true.

Some of the predictions made by Sweet Medicine were frightening, and he told of them as a warning to the Tse Tse Stus. He said that eventually, after many years, the Tse Tse Stus would not exist anymore, if we do not keep our traditional ways. He predicted that there would be only one language spoken by all the people of the earth. It would be then, he said, that the Cheyenne people would lose their language, traditions, and culture, that we would start to stray from the ways of Maheo—the Creator—and the ways that he taught us.

Sweet Medicine said that if we lost our traditions, bad things would start to happen to our people. Relatives would marry relatives, and our people would use things that would make them lose their minds. We would no longer think like Cheyenne. We would kill one another and go crazy. If this happens, if we allow ourselves to lose our culture, then the ve hoe will eventually destroy the earth with their technology.

Sweet Medicine eventually left the Tse Tse Stus. Throughout his life, from the time he was a child, Sweet Medicine changed the young buffalo calf hide that he wore with each season. With each of the four seasons, he hunted a young buffalo calf and skinned it carefully, so that the head and hooves would stay intact. One fall, he and other Tse Tse Stus men went out to hunt buffalo. It was time for him to kill a calf for his robe. During that hunt, a Cheyenne chief became jealous of Sweet Medicine and claimed for himself the young calf that Sweet Medicine had killed. This chief was not wise and was jealous of the powers Sweet Medicine possessed. He had been speaking badly of Sweet Medicine and had been spreading untrue rumors throughout the village. Angered, Sweet Medicine struck the chief. When the news of the fight reached the village, a meeting was held, and the jealous chief encouraged the Tse Tse Stus to banish Sweet Medicine from the tribe. After much discussion and argument, the others agreed.

The warriors, though, sided with Sweet Medicine. Upon hearing this news, Sweet Medicine became angry and told the people his final prediction. He told them of a young girl who will be pregnant for 20 years. When this girl finally gives birth to the child, it will be born an old man with yellow hair and sharp fangs. He will eat the Tse Tse Stus and we will no longer exist. With this, Sweet Medicine began walking away from the camp. A group of warriors chased after him, but every time they came to a ridge, Sweet Medicine was farther away. The warriors, though, ran faster and harder, and as they gained on him, he changed into a different animal and traveled even faster than before. The loyal warriors chased him for four days. On the fourth day, Sweet Medicine was gone, never to be heard from again. It has been said that he went up to the Sacred Mountain—Bear Butte—to die, and that is where he lies to this day, in a place no one knows. That place, today called Bear Butte, is still one of our most sacred places.

As Nam Shim remembered these stories and told them to Shadow, he could not help but think of the prophecies he had seen come true. Surely the white man were the people about whom Sweet Medicine had spoken. It was the white man who drank the water that burned their throats and raped their land with wagons, buildings, and other desecrations brought from the lands of the east. It was the white man who called the Tse Tse Stus "savages." Savages? Perhaps, but the "savagery" of which the Tse Tse Stus were guilty lay in their beliefs in honesty, bravery, and the chastity of their women.

These men were much different from Old Nam Shim's longtime friend Little White Man (Vé'ho'kĕso, or Skay ah veho), William Bent. His old friend understood the Tse Tse Stus ways, so well in fact that Little White Man married into the tribe. He married Owl Woman, daughter of the Keeper of the Sacred Medicine Arrows. This happened before Old Nam Shim was born. It happened when the land was still as The Wise One Above had made it and the only white men around were an insignificant number of Spaniards and a few "hair faces"—the mountain men who traded and lived in the lands of the Tse Tse Stus and Arapaho. These mountain men's days on the plains would soon be gone and so too would be the Tse Tse Stus.

For a brief instant, after his story had been told, Old Nam Shim silently wondered why The Wise One Above had stopped smiling on his people. To this day, Shadow remembers that silence, a silence that she broke when she implored Old Nam Shim, "Please tell me the story of the animals again. You know, the one about Mehn! Please, Nam Shim."

As her voice trailed off, the old man smiled and said, "Very well, Little One, for it, too, is a part of the story of the creation."

Discussion and Activities

Goals

■ Recount the Cheyenne creation story.

■ Identify who Sweet Medicine was, and discuss his prophecies.

Discussion Questions

1. Who was He'ámávé'ho'e?

    Answer: The Wise One Above, or the great spirit of the sky.

2. How many deities did the Cheyenne believe in, and who were they?

    Answer: Six. The spirits of the sky, the earth, and the four directions.

3. What animal found the earth in the great flood?

    Answer: The duck.

4. Is there such a thing as a "peace pipe"?

    Answer: No. The Cheyenne pipe was and is used in all of their ceremonies.

5. According to the Cheyenne, who taught them to make fire?

    Answer: The Wise One Above, or He'ámávé'ho'e.

6. Who was Sweet Medicine?

    Answer: A Cheyenne prophet.

7. Describe some of the predictions made by Sweet Medicine.

    Answer: The coming of the white man, the coming of the horse and cattle, the downfall of his people, the automobile, the airplane, and space travel.

8. Once the white man enters Cheyenne history, the Cheyenne's "reality" changes (pgs. 15–17). What changes occurred for the Cheyenne when Sweet Medicine's predictions had come to pass?

    (Teacher's note: Although not all of these changes are specifically discussed in the story, bring out some of these ideas to raise the awareness of students that the Cheyenne, as with all Native Americans, found their lives much changed after the arrival of the white man.)

    Answer: No longer was their existence tied to the old ways, to nature. With the white man came the horse; reservations; loss of freedom to practice their religious beliefs; and the introduction of white man's diseases, smallpox, measles, and cholera.

9. Read aloud the paragraph beginning "Shadow, all people are the same. . . ." (p. 14) In your own words, explain Nam Shim's meaning. Do you agree or disagree? Explain your answer.

Things to Do

Art Activity

Find a picture of a cottonwood tree and have the students draw it. Have students research how the cottonwood got its name and where it is found. Explain that wherever cottonwoods are found, water will be found, for the cottonwood is a thirsty tree. With this knowledge, the Cheyenne always knew where to find water.

Small Group Discussion

Have students look up the word *perspective*. Discuss how an event can be viewed differently by different people. It can be as basic as a case of an auto accident. There are always at least two versions. Have students brainstorm about how the white man and the Cheyenne felt about meeting each other. Divide the class into small groups. Instruct half of the groups to discuss the Cheyenne perspective, the other half to discuss the white man's perspective. Have each group write a short description of their thoughts. In a class discussion, have groups share the perspectives and discuss possible reasons for these viewpoints. The goal of this activity is to help students realize that the clash between these cultures, as in many other cases around the world, is about one culture viewing another from a different perspective but not giving value to the other's viewpoint. Discuss with students why it is difficult to change one's perspective and how this can produce misunderstanding, prejudice, and hatred.

Writing Activity

Using the information gathered in the discussion on perspectives (above), have each student choose the role of either the Native American or the white settler, and write a story about meeting someone from the other culture for the first time.

Library Research

All cultures have creation stories. Have students investigate the creation stories from other cultures (e.g., Chinese, Greek, Christian, Buddhist, etc.) and compare these to the Cheyenne creation story. Create a comparison chart for the cultures investigated and add it to the class bulletin board.

3

How the Animals and Other Things Came to Be

The Story of Mehn

"Please tell me the story of the animals again. You know, the one about Mehn! Please Nam Shim," Shadow implored.

The old man smiled and said, "Very well, Little One, for it, too, is a part of the story of the creation."

In the time of these stories, the warriors and medicine men all possessed great magical powers. And because the numbers four and seven are sacred to us, you will see that the deeds and things the people do are often performed four times, or that there are seven people or objects.

Did you know, Little One, that our people never camped out at the headwaters of any river? They believed that a terrible monster lived there and would kill and eat our people, especially our children. The monster's name was Mehn (Mé hne). Now, a long time ago there were two young Tse Tse Stus braves who were the best of friends. These two friends wanted to gain honor by counting coup, so they decided to take a journey together to do this and thereby gain the respect of their village. While on their quest, the two friends came to a deep, fast-running river. This river was so deep and fast that they were worried about crossing it safely. Standing on the river's bank, the first young brave looked at his friend and said, "I will cross first. I will call back to you and tell you how it is." His friend agreed and watched as the first brave swam across to the far bank. When the first brave had made it safely across, he waved to his friend. The second brave dove into the current and began to swim across. Suddenly, when he came to the middle of the river, he found that he couldn't move his legs. The brave on the far bank called out, "Hurry, we must go on!" The brave in the river called out, "I can't move. Something is holding me here. Go. Leave me."

At his friend's urging, the brave on the bank tried to continue on his journey alone. He left his friend and walked ahead but could not stop thinking of his best friend so bravely facing his fate in the river. He turned and went back to his friend. When he reached the river bank, he saw his friend in the current, just as he had left him. The brave in the river called out, "Go back to the camp and tell my parents that something has taken me. I shall never return."

Again the brave left him and started back to the Tse Tse Stus camp, but he couldn't bear to go on without his friend, so he again returned to the river, only to see that his friend had disappeared below the water. He walked up and down the bank for hours, crying and mourning for his lost friend.

Suddenly, a very old man appeared from behind the willows at the river's edge. He asked the young brave, "Why are you crying?"

The boy answered him, "Something has taken my friend below the surface of the river. I cannot bear to leave him behind, but I do not know what to do."

Upon hearing this news, the old man began to smile. The old man had long been searching for this thing that had taken the brave's friend. He explained to the brave that his friend had been taken by Mehn. He told him that Mehn was a rare creature who lives in the bottom of deep rivers and lakes. The old man said, "I have been hunting Mehn for many years, and you have helped me finally to find him. I am grateful." The old man told the brave many stories about Mehn, about how Mehn liked to lurk beneath the whirlpools of rivers, waiting for children to come swimming so he could take them and keep them beneath the surface. The old man told the boy that he had been hunting Mehn for its meat. He said that those who ate the delicious meat of Mehn would be strong and would surely live a long life.

The old man taught the young brave to beware of Mehn and how to listen for the low hissing sound that Mehn makes when he rises above the surface of the rivers. He told the brave to be careful if ever he were to see two lights near a river at night, for these lights are the eyes of Mehn, and this would mean that Mehn is hunting for people.

The brave and the old man made a plan to capture the creature and save the boy's friend. The old man instructed the brave, "Walk along the shore and cry loudly until your friend appears in the river. When you see him come up, say, 'I could not leave you. Come close to the shore and let me touch your hand once more before I go.' " The old man said that he would hide nearby in the willows because Mehn knew of the old man, and they were old enemies.

The brave agreed to the plan and began walking up and down the river's bank, crying for his friend. Soon, the brave in the river rose above the surface and said, "Are you still here? I told you to leave." He was worried that Mehn would capture his friend as well. The brave on the bank said to his friend, "Come close to the shore. Let me touch you." The brave in the river slowly moved closer to the shore until their hands touched. The brave on the shore grabbed his friend's hands tightly, and his friend yelled, "Let go of me!" With all his strength, the brave on the bank pulled until his friend broke free from the grip of Mehn—both braves landed on the bank of the river.

While Mehn was distracted and fighting to keep his hold on the brave, the old man, moving with the swiftness and strength of a much younger man, jumped into the river and attacked Mehn. The old man and Mehn fought ferociously in the water for a long time. Mehn would surface, making a great noise as the old man came up thrashing. Finally, after a long battle, the old man defeated the monster. Mehn slowly writhed in the water until he died. The old man triumphantly dragged Mehn's huge body from the river onto the shore, collapsing because of Mehn's size. The old man grinned a tired grin, satisfied that his long hunt was successful.

With Mehn dead, the three realized that the brave whom Mehn had captured could not move his legs. The old man explained to him that this always happens to any part of a human's body that Mehn touches.

"But Nam Shim," interrupted Shadow, "why didn't it happen to the old man? He touched Mehn!"

"This is true, Little One, but you must remember that the old man was more than just a man. He was a powerful medicine man."

Nam Shim continued his story as though he'd not been interrupted:

Pointing to a hill in the distance, the old man instructed the brave to carry his friend there and to look for a big rock at the top. He told him to stand in front of the rock and say, "Grandmother, hand me the robes for the sweat lodge. My friend needs a sweat bath." The brave did as he was told and watched as the big rock moved to one side to reveal an old woman standing in a large cave. The old woman greeted them and asked, "Why are you here?" The braves explained to her that the old man had sent them to get the robes for the sweat lodge. The old woman nodded, then turned and walked far into the cave. She soon returned with many soft and beautiful buffalo robes. The braves had never seen such robes. They thanked her and started back to the river's bank, one carrying the other.

The braves sat beside the river, the first brave exhausted from carrying his friend and the heavy robes. The two braves soon saw that the old man had set up the framework for the sweat lodge. Together, the first brave and the old man covered the frame with the buffalo robes, and the old man made preparations for a sweat. The old man made a great, hot fire outside the lodge; placed stones into the bed of hot, red coals; and then covered the ground inside the lodge with sage. He and the brave carried their injured friend into the lodge and laid him on the sage-covered ground. The old man brought in the hot stones using

deer antlers and sprinkled water on them, causing steam to rise and the lodge to become unbearably hot. After the sweat bath, the injured brave was able to walk again.

After this, the old man told the first brave to go back up the hill to the big rock and say, "Grandmother, open your door again." He told him to wait until the rock had moved to one side; when he could see the old woman, he was to say, "Grandfather wants his friends, the bears, to come and help him carry the meat of Mehn up the hill." The brave once again did as he had been told, and the old woman sent him back to the river with two huge brown bears. The brave had never seen such animals as these.

By the time the brave and the bears had returned to the river bank, the second brave and the old man had finished butchering Mehn. The bears then carried the meat, making many trips, up the hill to the old man's cave. The braves were surprised at the strength and the size of these strange, new animals.

When this work was done, the old man asked the two young braves to visit him in his home on the hill. They agreed and followed him up the hill to his cave. When the braves entered the cave, they were enchanted to see the most beautiful young girl they had ever seen standing near the old woman. This girl was the daughter of the old man and woman. The girl wore the skins and fur of creatures they had never before seen.

The old man was so thankful for the braves' help in capturing Mehn that he gave them his daughter. The girl and the brave that had been caught by Mehn immediately fell in love, and soon after, they married. The braves lived with the old man and woman for some time but became worried about their families and tribe that they had left behind. They told the old man, "We must go back to our tribe." Everyone agreed.

As the braves and the young girl were packing to leave, the old man told the braves again how thankful he was for their help in capturing Mehn. He wanted to give them a special gift to take home to their people. The old man motioned for something in back of him to come forward. With this, all forms of animals appeared from behind the old man: buffalo, bear, coyote, fish, beaver, turtle, deer, elk, and many others the braves had never before seen. The old man said, "These are my friends, the animals. I give them to you and your people as a token of my gratitude."

As the three were leaving, the old man took his daughter aside and said to her, "You must not feel sad when these people kill our friends for food. You must never say these words: My poor pets (Na'shi-vatúmnátutse). Now go!"

When the two braves and the girl arrived at their village, all the people were happy to see them. The braves were proud to bring home to their village such wondrous gifts as animals. The village had been without food for many days. As the buffalo saw this, they felt pity for the Tse Tse Stus, and they gave themselves to the people, telling the people to kill them. The buffalo told the people how to prepare their meat and use their skins and bones for useful things. As the young girl watched the buffalo being killed, she forgot what her father had told her and said, "My poor pets."

The next morning when her husband awoke, he found that his wife had disappeared. She was never seen again.

"Nam Shim, where did she go?" asked Shadow.

"Child, we Tse Tse Stus have many stories in which a medicine man, such as the old man in this story, instructs a person not to utter certain words or phrases. In all cases, if the person disobeys, they disappear and are never heard from again. So no one really knows where she went. Maybe the Creator cast her up into the sky as he did those boys."

"What boys?" implored Shadow.

Nam Shim did this to her often. One story would be a perfect lead into another story, and it was in this way that he held her attention for hours. Their daily walks and talks would always end with a storytelling session. Old Nam Shim would point out many of Mother Nature's wonders and tell Shadow the story behind each of them.

"The story I will tell you about these boys explains many wonders of our world—some that you have seen and others you have not.

The Big Dipper, the Bear, and the Devil's Tower

Once there was a girl who was an only child. Her mother tanned a bear skin for her, and the girl liked it very much. The girl used to sit and sleep on it. She was so fond of the robe that she took it everywhere she went.

One day the girl took her robe and went up to a hill to quill. While she sat there quilling, seven brothers came up to her and asked her to play with them. The game they wanted to play had to do with a bear. The girl said, "I'm busy quilling. I am too busy to play your game." The boys kept insisting until finally, out of frustration, she consented.

The boys told her to wrap herself in her robe and pretend to be a bear. She put on her robe over her shoulders as the boys held hands in a line. The oldest brother was the first line of protection against the "bear." The girl began to chase them. At first the game seemed innocent enough, but soon the girl began to act more and more like a real bear. The boys became scared as the game wore on, thinking she had become a real bear. They noticed that the girl's hands had claws, and that she looked just like a bear.

The oldest brother said, "Let's run away!" All the boys were good runners, but they knew that they were out of sight of the village. Besides, the bear was between them and their village, so they ran even farther from the village. As they ran, they could see her chasing them.

The youngest brother became very tired and said he couldn't run anymore. The boys stopped to let him rest, and the oldest brother said, "Sometimes when I play alone, I make cactus grow, and it protects me."

When he said this, cactus began growing all around them. They now had time to rest and watch the bear because she couldn't get to them through the cactus. Once they had rested, the boys began running again. Behind them they could hear the bear call out, "Wait for me!" She had made her way around the cactus and was now gaining on the boys. Again the youngest brother became tired, and they had to stop to rest.

The oldest brother said, "When I play alone, I make the bushes grow to protect me, so that nothing can get to me." When he said this, bushes began growing everywhere between the boys and the bear. They rested again while the bear tried to get through the bushes. As she tried, she kept calling out for the boys to wait for her.

After they had rested, they began running, and again the bear made her way through the barrier of bushes and began gaining on the boys. The youngest brother became tired a third time, and the boys stopped to rest. The oldest brother said, "When I play alone and I need protection from something that scares me, I play as though there is a wash." No sooner had

Doll

he said this than a huge wash appeared behind them, and the bear couldn't get across. As the bear came close to the wash, she begged the resting boys to help her across. They were too frightened to help her, so they just watched her as she begged.

Soon after, the boys began running again, and as they ran and looked back, they could see that the bear had made her way across the wash and was gaining on them.

For a fourth time, the youngest brother became tired and could no longer run. When they stopped, the oldest brother said, "When I play alone sometimes and I need protection from something that's after me, I play as though there is a high rock for me to climb." Instantly, the large, flat rock on which the boys had been standing became a high rock.

Devil's Tower, located in Wyoming

The bear approached and tried to jump up on the rock. All the brothers were afraid. The oldest boy said, "Be quiet! She will think she is powerful, but we will get away. She will never reach us! When I play, I pray that the rock will grow higher and higher." As he said these words, the rock grew.

The bear jumped at the rock but fell, unable to get a grip on it. Her claws made scratch marks along the face of the rock. The rock grew higher and higher until it was more than 1,000 feet tall. The boys were unable to get down, but the Creator took pity on the boys and cast them up into the sky, where they became the seven stars of the Big Dipper. The bear was also cast up into the sky as a constellation, and the rock the boys stood on became the Devil's Tower.

Sometimes, Shadow, our stories tell of the individual adventures of these brothers. This next one is about Ma Guss. His name means "The Youngest."

Ma Guss (The Youngest)

There once was a little boy by the name of Ma Guss (Ma'kŏ'se). He had six brothers and one sister. He was about eight years old, the youngest child in his family. The six brothers often went hunting together, but before they left, they would always tell Ma Guss not to wander and to watch his older sister. One day Ma Guss said to his sister, "Make me a bow and arrow. I have seen birds close by, and I want to shoot them." The girl made him a bow and arrow.

When the older brothers found out that Ma Guss had a bow and arrows, they became worried about him. They were afraid he would wander away while hunting. They told him not to wander away because Hupéneohótauh'e, who was a powerful and evil buffalo medicine man, often traveled near their campsite. They didn't want Hupéneohótuah'e near their sister because he might steal her. Ma Guss promised he wouldn't leave his sister. Then the brothers left again.

When the sister went for water, Ma Guss went with her, but Ma Guss began chasing a bird and wandered too far. Hupéneohótuah'e had been watching the sister for many days and was waiting for her. He caught her and took her with him.

When Ma Guss returned home, he found her gone. He went to the river to look for her. All he found was a water bag.

Ma Guss followed her tracks. He found two sets of tracks going upriver, and he knew that Hupéneohótuah'e had her. He went home, feeling guilty because his brothers had told him to watch his sister, and he hadn't. He blamed himself.

The brothers returned one at a time. As each returned, he asked, "Where is our sister? We told you to look after her. Where is she?" Ma Guss, feeling bad, told each brother, "I guess she went with Hupéneohótuah'e." He had his head hung down when he said this to each brother.

A few days after she disappeared, Ma Guss said, "I am going to look for our sister, and I will bring her back." The brothers said, "You will never get her back because Hupéneohótuah'e is very strong. He has powerful medicine, and you can do nothing."

Ma Guss became stubborn and said, "I don't care if he is powerful. I'll get her back." Before he left, he said to his brothers, "While I am gone, build four fences around the camp and make many arrows. I don't know how long I'll be gone." He left, and the six brothers began building the fences. Ma Guss came to where he could see a first camp. He sat upon a hill above the camp watching some kids playing. He went down and began playing with them. He noticed one boy in particular and played with him. By the way this boy did things and played, Ma Guss could tell that the boy had been raised by an old woman. Ma Guss switched spirits with the boy—he put his spirit into the boy's body—and walked into the grandmother's lodge. He said to the old woman, "Grandma, I am very hungry."

"Help yourself," she said. "I made some pemmican."

Ma Guss sat down and began eating the pemmican. He said, "Grandma, have you heard any special news?"

She said, "People are talking about Hupéneohótuah'e. He passed through our village, and he had a wife with him. People are saying that she was the sister of the seven brothers."

Ma Guss said, "The heck with that Hupéneohótuah'e!"

"Hush!" said the old woman. "Don't say a thing like that. He is a medicine man and he might hear you. The ground is his ears, so don't ever say anything about him again."

Ma Guss again said, "The heck with that Hupéneohótuah'e!" The grandmother again begged him not to say anything. Ma Guss said, "I'm going out to play again," and he walked out of the lodge. As he left, he again switched spirits with the boy he'd met.

He started walking away from the village. He walked all day and slept out that night. He walked another day, and that night came to a second camp. He again watched from a hill for children he could play with. He saw a poor little boy and played with him for awhile. Ma Guss switched spirits with this boy and went into his lodge, where he found an old woman. He said to the old woman, "Grandma, I'm very hungry."

"Help yourself," said the old woman. "I just made some pounded meat." As Ma Guss was eating, he asked the old woman, "Has anything interesting happened in the village?" She told him the same thing as had the woman in the previous village.

Ma Guss again said, "To heck with Hupéneohótuah'e!"

The old woman said, "Don't say anything about him. He is a medicine man." Again Ma Guss said he was going out to play and walked out. As he left this village, he again switched spirits with the boy.

He walked again and came to a third village. Again he sat upon a hill and looked down. This time he knew that he had caught up with Hupéneohótuah'e and his sister.

He went down and played with the children and again switched spirits with a boy who had been raised by an old woman. He went into their lodge and said, "Grandma, I am very hungry."

She said, "Your food is ready, and you can eat."

As he was eating, he asked her, "Has anything happened in camp?"

She said, "Hupéneohótuah'e just arrived with his new wife. His wife is the sister of the seven brothers."

Ma Guss asked, "Where are they camping?"

"They are in the lodge way at the end, facing the other way," she said.

Ma Guss said, "I'm going out to play again."

As it became dark outside, he played closer to Hupéneohótuah'e's lodge. He peeked under the back of the lodge. There he saw Hupéneohótuah'e sitting with his sister. All around the lodge were old men smoking the pipe. Ma Guss put down the flaps of the lodge, thus closing the opening to the outside. He hid where he could hear Hupéneohótuah'e talking. Hupéneohótuah'e said to his wife, "You go out and fix the flap to stay up."

She came outside and saw Ma Guss. She said, "What are you doing here? You should not have come."

Ma Guss said, "I have come for you."

"It's no use," she said.

Ma Guss told her, "When you go back inside, I will put down the flap again. Then, when you come out again and fix it, bring your robe." He put down the flap again.

When she entered the lodge again, Hupéneohótuah'e said to her, "Go out and fix the flap." She did so, taking her robe with her. Ma Guss told her to put her robe behind the lodge. He also told her to pull out one strand of hair and put it on top of the robe.

After she did this, Ma Guss said, "We had better go now."

Back inside the lodge, Hupéneohótuah'e kept saying, "Hurry and fix the flap and come in."

"Wait," said the girl from outside the lodge.

Hupéneohótuah'e repeated his command three times, and three times she said "Wait." The fourth time he said he was going to come out and get her. After the fourth time she told him to wait, Hupéneohótuah'e got mad and went outside to get her. He saw her sitting where she had left the robe. He said, "What are you doing out here? I told you to come in a long time ago." He picked her up, but what he had put his arms around was just the robe and one hair.

Hupéneohótuah'e went inside and told the old men, "She's gone. She left."

By this time, Ma Guss and his sister were quite a ways from the camp. Ma Guss told his sister, "Close your eyes." Then he said, "Now you can open them." When she did, they were very near their own camp.

On their fourth day away from home, as Ma Guss and his sister walked toward the camp, their six brothers were watching for them. Ma Guss told his brothers, "I have brought our sister back as I promised you." The four fences were ready. The six brothers had also made plenty of arrows as Ma Guss had told them.

After they had been home one day, they saw a herd of buffalo calves walking toward the camp. One came into the camp to talk to Ma Guss. The calf said, "Hupéneohótuah'e sent us to get his wife."

Ma Guss replied, "You go back and tell him that I will not let my sister go." The calf went back to Hupéneohótuah'e.

The next day, a herd of yearling buffalo came, and one of them said, "Hupéneohótuah'e sent us to get his wife. If you don't give her up, Hupéneohótuah'e will attack."

Ma Guss said, "I am not sending my sister back, and you can tell him to attack."

The third day, more buffalo came and said, "Hupéneohótuah'e is going to attack."

Ma Guss said, "Let him attack. I am not sending my sister back."

The sister begged Ma Guss, "Let me go back."

Ma Guss said, making fun of Hupéneohótuah'e, "He's not fit to be your husband."

One buffalo calf said, "This time Hupéneohótuah'e is really going to attack."

Then the first buffalo calves that had warned them attacked, tearing down the first fence, but the six brothers killed them all with arrows. The second group of yearlings attacked and tore down the second fence, and again the brothers killed them. The girl became frightened when she saw this and again begged, "Let me go back. Please let me go. They are going to kill us. There are a lot of them, and you can't kill them all."

Ma Guss said, "No, you can't go back." The third herd attacked and tore down the third fence, but the six brothers killed them also. All the buffalo lay dead, their bodies scattered about. Hupéneohótuah'e was the only one left standing. Hupéneohótuah'e did all sorts of powerful things. He stomped on the ground—it cracked and made a blue flash.

How the Animals and Other Things Came to Be

Again the girl begged, "Let me go back. He is powerful, and we can't do anything. He is a medicine man and will kill us all."

Ma Guss said, making fun of Hupéneohótuah'e, "Be quiet. To me he means nothing. He is just doing all this to show off his power, but his medicine is not that powerful. You, my sister, are the only one around here who is afraid of your husband. He must have made up his own medicine. I am more powerful than Hupéneohótuah'e, and I can destroy him." His sister was quiet after this.

Enraged, Hupéneohótuah'e transformed himself into a huge bull buffalo and charged, tearing the fourth fence to pieces. The pieces flew all over. All of a sudden, the sister was sitting on top of a very tall tree. Ma Guss, using his powers, had put her there to protect her. Hupéneohótuah'e backed up and began charging the tree. The third time he charged, he began to split the tree. Then, with a blue flash, he split the tree to the top. Hupéneohótuah'e had only enough power left for one more charge. His brothers were out of arrows, but Ma Guss had one arrow left. Ma Guss ordered the six brothers to get into the tree. Again, the girl begged, "Let me come down, and I will go back to him."

Ma Guss, astonished by Hupéneohótuah'e's power, said, "Where is this medicine man from?" Ma Guss chewed on his last arrow and took aim. His aim was true—and he shot Hupéneohótuah'e through the heart. After Hupéneohótuah'e fell, he said to Ma Guss, "You killed me," and then he died.

After his brothers had climbed down, Ma Guss told them to gather wood, and they did so. They built a fire, pulled Hupéneohótuah'e into it, and burned him. After the coals had died down, there were many beads of different colors lying where Hupéneohótuah'e had been.

Ma Guss told his brothers and sister not to pick them up, no matter how pretty they looked.

The brothers butchered the other buffalo, and the girl made dry meat. She sliced the meat, and the boys hung it on poles in the camp.

Ma Guss knew that the main camp, where he and his brothers and sister were from, was hungry. After they had finished making dry meat, Ma Guss found a chunk of buffalo fat. He called a raven, and it came to him. He told the raven to take the fat and drop it into the main camp.

The raven was a messenger. As he flew over the camp, he said, "You have forgotten about the seven brothers, but here is something they give to you."

The people picked up the fat, and the raven led the whole village to the hunting camp of the seven brothers. Ma Guss told the people to camp where the dried meat was, and that each could have what was near their lodge. Everyone was happy after being fed. Then the brothers and their sister cast themselves up into the heavens. They are still there, shining every night in the shape of the Big Dipper.

Discussion and Activities

Goals

■ Become familiar with examples of the legends and stories from the Cheyenne culture.

Discussion Questions

1. Who or what was Mehn, and why were children afraid of him?

   Answer: A monster that lived in the deep, fast-running water at the headwater of rivers. It is said that he ate children.

2. What happened to the Cheyenne brave in the river?

   Answer: Mehn captured him.

3. How was the brave rescued from Mehn?

   Answer: An old man, who was hunting Mehn for its meat, helped rescue the boy and killed Mehn.

4. How did the old man thank the braves for helping him kill Mehn?

   Answer: He healed the injured brave's leg and gave the braves all the animals in nature to take to their people so that they might hunt them.

5. Why were the animals so important to the Tse Tse Stus?

   Answer: Animals are a source of food; the Tse Tse Stus would not have to worry about starving.

6. Why was the old man's daughter instructed never to say "My poor pets"?

   Answer: So the Cheyenne would not know of her sadness when the animals were killed for food.

7. What happened to the old man's daughter when she disobeyed his command?

   Answer: She disappeared.

8. Who teased the girl with the bear-skin robe to come play?

   Answer: Seven brothers.

9. What were the four things the boys used to slow down the bear?

   Answer: Cactus, a forest, a wash that turned into a canyon, and a large rock.

10. What did the rock become, and what happened to the seven brothers and the girl who turned into the bear?

    Answer: The rock became the Devil's Tower, the boys became the stars of the Big Dipper, and the bear became the bear constellation.

11. Who was Ma Guss?

    Answer: The youngest of the seven brothers. His name means "the youngest."

12. What happened that forced Ma Guss on a quest to find Hupéneohótuah'e?

> ***Answer:*** His sister was kidnapped by Hupéneohótuah'e. Ma Guss had been told to watch his sister because of this danger, so he felt it was his responsibility to rescue her.

13. What special power did Ma Guss have?

> ***Answer:*** He could switch spirits with other boys and ask questions in their camps for information.

14. What happened after Ma Guss rescued his sister?

> ***Answer:*** Hupéneohótuah'e, the evil buffalo medicine man, sent out herds of buffalo to kill Ma Guss and his brothers. The brothers had built four fences and made arrows for protection. In the end, Ma Guss killed the medicine man with his last arrow.

Things to Do

Writing Activity

With the class, compare some of the classic "boogie man" stories with the story of Mehn. Discuss with students what the purpose of this type of story might be (e.g., a method of discipline—certainly, telling children about Mehn would keep them away from the dangers of the river). Have students write about a "boogie man" story they have been told. Have each student share their story and discuss its purpose.

Creative Writing/Art Activity

Examine a map of the constellations with your class. Have students choose a constellation and write their own myth about the origin of the constellation. To illustrate their story, have students draw their constellation with white chalk on black construction paper. "Fix" the chalk with a spray pastel fixative (available at art and craft stores). Display the constellations and have students share their myths.

Food: Jerky

Because there was no other way to preserve the meat of buffalo, the Cheyenne would dry it, making jerky. Discuss this method of food preservation with students. If a food dehydrator is available, arrange to make jerky in the classroom. There are a number of recipes available. Most students have probably tried beef jerky, but try to find recipes for other dried meats (e.g., fish).

Library Research

Many cultures have mythologies that explain the origins of the constellations (some of the better known are of Greek origin). Have students research the various constellations and the myths about how they came to be. Have students share the stories they find. Discuss with the class the similarities and differences.

Class Bulletin Board

On a map, locate Devil's Tower.

Ann Strange Owl-Raben (in her mother's mother's dress)

4

How the Cheyenne Got Horses

"*Now, Shadow, I want to tell you a tale that was told by our old ones a long time ago. It took place in what is now southeastern Colorado. There, not too far from the place called Sand Creek (Póénẽõ ó'he'e), is a river called the River of Lost Souls in Purgatory. Do you remember what the Catholic missionaries said Purgatory is?*"

"*No, Nam Shim,*" *said Shadow, "they haven't taught me that yet.*"

Well, child, it is a place in their religion where the soul must stay as a temporary punishment until the sins they committed on earth have been atoned for. Yet many years ago, this river was not the picture of gloom and despair that its name implies. Elk foraged in thickets of huge sunflowers, and wild turkeys, black bears, and deer competed for succulent wild plums and cherries. In this land, blackbirds perched on cattails filled the air with their calls, while giant cottonwoods, gnarled with age, lined either side of a river whose slow, surging waters gave life to the prairie itself. In its beauty, this rich bottomland offered refuge from the scorching heat of summer.

When summer turned to autumn, and wildflowers blossomed in profusion, giant grizzly bears arrived to hunt buffalo. Their savage power was something to behold. These 1,200-pound bruins could chase down a young buffalo with bursts of speed as fast as a running horse. Yet, in their more docile and lethargic moments, they feasted on chokecherries and other delicacies before retiring to a winter's sleep. This land of plenty was also home to cougars, wolves, prairie chickens, and great herds of antelope. However, there was more here than merely a gathering of the food chain. This land functioned for our people as a natural oasis and as a windbreak against the harshness of winter's snows.

Our people knew well the mouth of that river. Legends of tragedy and death were born there. Our people and Spaniards alike related a story about this river's mouth. Before the Tse Tse Stus possessed horses, it is said that a group of our boys were out playing in the prairie some distance from their village. All of a sudden, they saw something that frightened and amazed them. What they saw were monsters! There were 30 of them, and they had four legs, two heads, and a tail. Every once in a while, one of the monsters would reach up and take off one of its heads. After watching this for a time, the frightened boys ran back to the village and told everyone what they had seen.

Most everyone in the village thought the boys to be touched in the head from being out in the hot sun for so long, but the elders believed that the boys had seen something. The elders told the fastest warriors in the village to follow the boys' trail and go see what was there. Reluctantly, they agreed.

The warriors ran, following the boys' tracks until they no longer saw any tracks. The warriors stopped, but one decided to go farther, continuing in the same direction from where the boys had come. Lo and behold, to his astonishment, the warrior found tracks of an animal he had never seen. He called out to his friends, and they, too, saw these strange tracks. He told one of his friends to return to the village, to tell the others what they had found, and to ask for more warriors. This the warrior did, and the others continued following the tracks of these animals until, finally, they too saw the monsters upon a knoll, silhouetted against the setting sun. And yes, they had four legs, two heads, and a tail! As they got closer, though, the warriors saw that these were not monsters at all, but a new kind of man riding on a magnificent four-legged animal. What they saw were the Spanish Conquistadors, who had been sent by their leaders in Mexico to suppress all the Indians beyond the borders of Spain's new empire. The Spaniards called our people Indians because when Columbus landed in the New World, he thought he was in India. Yet the sight of these curious men with "iron bellies" (armor) on these four-legged beasts intrigued our people. One of the warriors said that these men and animals were the ones mentioned in Sweet Medicine's prophecy. The warriors' curiosity and Conquistador arrogance proved to be the catalysts that forever changed the course of Western history.

Once these Spaniards succeeded in their mission, the leaders disobeyed their orders to return to Mexico and chose instead to explore new lands. The age-old struggle for supreme glory, however, erupted between the two leaders of the expedition. During an argument one night, they fought a duel to the death. The priests, who were always present on those expeditions, told the remainder of the troops to abandon their campaign, for they now believed it to be cursed by God. Undaunted by the priests' warning and without their blessing, Spain's conquerors continued on into the unknown vastness of the Great Plains. Unafraid of the increasing number of Tse Tse Stus they encountered along the way, the Spaniards journeyed until they came to the mouth of a river.

On the evening of their arrival, they set up camp. Confident about their superiority over any "savage," the Spaniards posted no sentries. Surely, they thought, these "root grubbers" could do no harm. Had not Pizarro, with only 160 men, conquered the Incan army of 80,000 men in Peru? And had they not heard of Cabeza de Vaca's eight-year, 6,000-mile journey, following Indian trails and living off the land? During his odyssey, de Vaca himself wrote about the mild and friendly tribes he and his three companions had encountered.

This was not the last time that underestimating these natives would end in disaster. While those from Spain slept, Tse Tse Stus crept into their camp and started a grass fire. In the confusion, they stole the horses and killed the "iron bellies." Two exceptions were a mulatto slave girl and a lone Conquistador. Because this Conquistador fought with such ferocity, the Tse Tse Stus spared his life. His knowledge of the horse, they knew, would be invaluable. Legends from both the Tse Tse Stus and the Spanish tell of this Conquistador's elevation to a great chief of the Tse Tse Stus tribe.

Our people spoke of this battle as "the time in which we got horses." The Spaniards, however, spoke of their men who died at the mouth of that river. According to the Spanish tale, the souls of the Conquistadors were doomed forever, for they died without receiving the last rites of the Catholic Church. Since those days long ago, Child, legends say these lost souls in Purgatory have dwelled upon the banks of the river now called Purgatory.

"After we got horses, our people became great horsemen, and as the pony herds grew, so did our knowledge of these great animals. Shadow, do you know how we Cheyenne broke wild horses?"

"Like you see in the rodeo?" asked Shadow. "Bucking broncos?"

"No. We found out a long time ago that horses will not buck if they are standing in a river. Our warriors would rope them, using rope made from the long hair of a horse's tail and mane. They would then get a horse into a river and mount him. After walking him around in the river awhile to get him used to having weight on his back, our warriors would start to lead him out of the water. If the horse started to buck, the warrior would strike the horse between the eyes with his riding crop and guide the horse back into the river. After repeating this a couple of times, the horse got the idea. It didn't take long to break a wild horse."

Discussion and Activities

Goals

■ Become familiar with the traditional story of how the Cheyenne obtained horses.

■ Learn the Spanish version of the same story.

■ Describe the land in southeastern Colorado 350 years ago.

■ Describe the first meeting of the Cheyenne and the white man.

Discussion Questions

1. Name at least four animals in the story that no longer live in the plains of southeastern Colorado. Speculate as to why they have disappeared from this region.

    Answer: Grizzly bear, cougar, wolves, elk, buffalo, and prairie chickens. With the coming of more and more people, particularly the white man, and with the building of more towns and roads, the animals were hunted to extinction in this area, or they moved into other areas.

2. What did the young Cheyenne boys think they saw when they first spotted the Conquistadors?

    Answer: Monsters—with two heads, four legs, and a tail. In describing the men dismounting their horses, the boys said that they had seen the monsters take off one of their heads.

3. What did the Cheyenne warriors do when they caught up with the Conquistadors?

    Answer: They followed them to the mouth of a river. There, they killed the Conquistadors and took the horses, animals they had never before seen.

4. How did the River of Lost Souls in Purgatory get its name?

    Answer: From this incident when the Spanish Conquistadors died at the mouth of this river in southeastern Colorado (El Rio de Las Animas Perdidas en Purgatorio). The Spaniards claim that the souls of those men were doomed to Purgatory because they had not received the last rites of the Catholic Church.

5. The Cheyenne learned to work with horses very quickly, and they soon became expert horsemen. Where did the Cheyenne go to break a horse?

    Answer: A river. The Cheyenne learned that horses won't buck if they are in water.

Things to Do

Art Activity

Have students find pictures and descriptions of prairies. They should pay special attention to the wildlife, vegetation, and the colors that are present in a prairie. Working in small groups or as a class, have students create one or several murals depicting a prairie landscape. Add these art projects to the class bulletin board.

Have students draw favorite scenes from the narrative of this chapter. Add these to the class bulletin board.

Library Research

Have students research the Conquistadors: How did they first come to the New World? Where did they first land? Have students trace their movements into North America on a map. Add this map to the class bulletin board.

The horse was not native to the Americas, but brought here by the Spaniards. Have students research the history of the horse and how the Spaniards transported these animals.

Class Bulletin Board

On the map of the Conquistador movements into North America, have students locate the approximate place where the Cheyenne first met the Conquistadors and the River of Lost Souls in Purgatory (Purgatory River).

Brainstorm with the class about all the ways the horse might change the way the Cheyenne lived. Make a list of these changes in chart form and add it to the class bulletin board.

5

Stories of Magic and Medicine Men

Girl-Horse

*A*s the years passed, Shadow listened with great anticipation for the next story that Old Nam Shim would tell. She loved horses and horse stories and remembered one story in particular. One night, when she was 10 years old—and Old Nam Shim had completed 10 times that number of years in his life—he told Shadow this story:

There was once a girl who was an only child. Her parents loved her very much. She was beautiful and a good worker and quiller. Her camp was large, and it was moved a lot because the young men in her village wanted to count coup on their enemies.

One morning, after breaking camp, the girl discovered she had lost her favorite awl, the one her father had made for her.

She said, "Mother, I forgot my awl. I will go back and get it."

"Leave it," her mother said. "Your father will make another."

But the girl liked the awl so much that she went back anyway. This worried the women in the camp, so they decided to wait for her. They waited until the tribal leaders insisted they come with the rest of the people.

Now this girl had a very fast horse, and when she came to where she had left her awl, she dismounted to pick it up. As she did, a great wild stallion came running down the hill and chased her horse away. The stallion turned, from a distance, and looked at the girl. He had never seen such a beautiful human being before, and he charged down the hill again and took her away.

Close-up of beadwork on lodge liner

On the first day of the camp's new journey, the tribe decided to wait for the girl for one day and one night, but she didn't return. The next morning, the father said to his wife, "Come on. We will look for our daughter. We will find her and then catch up to the rest of the people later." When the parents returned to the old campground, the only thing they found was her horse. All the girl's belongings were still on the horse, which was restless.

The father freed the girl's horse, and it led him and his wife to a herd of wild horses. As the parents watched the horses, they noticed the powerful stallion and their daughter in the middle of the herd. When the stallion saw the girl's parents, he chased away the herd. The girl went with the herd, so the father chased them. But his horse tired, and he had to turn back.

He told his wife that he couldn't catch them. The father said he thought that the stallion had taken their daughter, but that the stallion was too powerful for him alone. So they returned to the main camp to get the young men to help.

The young men and the parents returned to the herd, and when they saw the girl, they discovered that her body had turned into a horse, but her head was still the same. The girl-horse looked at her parents, but the stallion chased her and the herd away. The young men chased the herd, but their horses tired. They returned to camp to get fresh horses.

Again they chased the herd, and this time the young men caught the girl-horse.

As they brought her to her father, she pleaded, "I have turned into a horse, and people will only make fun of me. Leave me here. You can always visit me."

The father said, "She is right. Turn her loose." To his daughter he said, "We will return to see you. When we do, come away from the herd and see us."

When they returned to the main camp, the father announced what had happened, and everyone pitied him and his wife.

When the parents became lonesome, they would return to see their daughter. One day, her parents saw her with two colts. The colts were her children. She came away from the herd and talked to her parents. This time, though, she told her parents never to come again. "It is no use," she said. "I can never turn back into a human again, nor can I come back to our people. I know that these visits only hurt your feelings. Always remember that I am not dead."

Many years later, the parents went to see her but didn't talk to her. She was running wild and free with the herd. When she saw her parents, she came away from the herd so they would know it was she. It was the last time they ever saw her.

"Nam Shim, that's a sad story," said Shadow. "I don't understand what lesson could be in that story."

"Shadow, think about it. All stories have lessons in them. Think about what happened from beginning to end."

Shadow paused awhile and thought. "Maybe she should have listened to her mother before she did something so dangerous?" she said, questioning Nam Shim.

"Very good, Little One, and the fact that, at the time, the girl did not think it was dangerous. The story also says that this girl-horse took responsibility for her own actions. When it was too late to become a human again, she continued on as a horse. Most important, this story says that sometimes, when one acts on sudden impulses, it can have terrible effects on the feelings and lives of loved ones.

"Now, Shadow, you must understand that for nearly every story of tragedy there is a story about a great hero or a medicine man. The story of the girl-horse is one of disobedience that ended in sadness. This next story is one of disobedience that a father used to test his son's greatness. The son's name was His Stah."

"Nam Shim, doesn't that mean 'Belly Button'?" asked Shadow. "Why would the father call him such a funny name?"

"Shadow, the story itself will answer that for you. This is a story of how a great medicine man came to be."

His Stah (Belly Button)

During a summer not so long ago, a group of Tse Tse Stus had set up a small hunting camp away from the main camp. At this camp, where only a few lodges (éŝkȯseome) were set up, a man and his wife were expecting the birth of their first child. One day, just as the man was riding into camp from a hunting expedition, his wife was giving birth to a baby boy. Afterwards, the father took the placenta down to the river, threw it in, and watched as it floated downstream.

As the years passed and the boy grew, the family returned to the same place each summer and set up a camp for hunting. Each spring, the boy longed to return to the camp where he could go down to the river's bank and play. One day while he was playing by the river, he met another boy who looked as if he could be a twin brother. This boy had been waiting at the river for the family to return each summer; this mysterious twin was actually the placenta that the father had thrown into the river a few summers before. He had become a person (vo'ėstane).

Every day the boy's mother heard her son playing and talking to someone down by the river, but she knew that he was the only child at the hunting camp and thought that he was just entertaining himself, perhaps with an imaginary playmate. Finally, though, she became curious, and one morning she decided to follow her son. While quietly hiding behind a willow, she watched as her son played with this boy who looked as if he were a twin brother. The boy from the river sensed that he was being watched and immediately dove back into the river and disappeared below the surface.

That evening, when the father returned from hunting, the boy's mother related to him what had happened. Both parents were curious about their son's new friend and wondered if this strange boy might possibly have been born from their son's placenta even though this had never happened before. The father knew that the river boy was shy and wary of anyone but their son, so he devised a plan. First he braided a cord made of sinew, then he attached this cord to a float fashioned from the intestines of a buffalo. He and his wife waited until their son had gone down to the river to play. Quietly, they followed him and hid in the willow on the bank. When the river boy came out to play, the father quickly jumped from the willows and struggled to tie the float to him. The river boy fought him and cried to be let loose. When the float was secure, the father let him go and watched as the river boy dove into the water. The river boy tried and tried to dive down below the surface, but the float held his head above water.

The father told his son, "Son, try to talk to your friend. Ask him to come and live with us. I know now that he is your placenta, which I threw in the river after you were born. He is my son, just as you are." The son talked to the river boy, telling him that he was welcome in their lodge. The river boy had been lonely without a family, and he agreed to go with them.

The two brothers quickly became inseparable. The mother and father named the river boy His Stah (Hésta'he). The father knew that His Stah was special in some way. He thought that perhaps his second son had the powers of a medicine man. He tested His Stah by telling him not to do certain things, knowing that His Stah could not resist the challenge.

One day, before going hunting, the father warned his sons, "Up in those hills there are many snakes. Do not go up there."

Both boys nodded their heads and replied, "Yes, Father," but as soon as the man rode off, His Stah turned to his brother and said, "Let's go up into those hills and see the snakes." Of course, his brother, who wasn't as smart, always agreed. His Stah and his brother went up into the hills and found the snakes. They captured many rattlesnakes and took off their rattles.

Picking up the rattles, His Stah said, "Let's play a joke on our father. He is going to bring home some meat today. I will put these rattles in our heads before we go back home and when we eat the meat, the rattles in our heads will rattle like a snake." So His Stah emptied their heads and put in the rattles. All the way down the hill the brothers laughed as their heads rattled like snakes.

When the boys arrived, their father had already returned to camp. He saw them coming and heard the rattles in their heads. He knew then that His Stah was powerful, but he frowned and said to them, "I told you boys not to go up to the snake den in those hills, but you disobeyed me! Now go back up there and give those rattles back." The boys went back up into the hills, and there His Stah and his brother took the rattles from their heads and put them back on the snakes.

The next day as the father was again getting ready to leave camp, he gave his sons another warning. He asked them to come into the lodge where he told them not to go near the home of the thunderbird. He told them that at this particular time of the year, it is dangerous to go near the birds' nests because they are guarding their young. He said, "The thunderbirds have small ones, and the mother birds are mean. They will attack you if you go near their nests."

The boys promised not to go near the nests. The father rode off again to hunt, and His Stah turned to his brother and said, "Let's go up to the thunderbird nests." And again, of course, the brother agreed. The boys had to travel farther this time, and they climbed for a long time before they finally reached the place of the thunderbirds. Once they had reached the nests, they began taking the baby birds and stuffing them into their shirts. The mother birds flew at them, attacking. His Stah was unharmed, but his brother was killed. His Stah reached over to touch him, and he came back to life. This happened more than once. Each time His Stah helped his brother up, he would say, "You are not very strong—you die easily." Each time the birds attacked, the boy would be killed, and His Stah grew weary of reviving him.

While this was going on, the father had returned to camp early and noticed that the boys were gone. He looked up towards the thunderbird nests, saw the thunderbirds attacking, and realized that the boys had once again disobeyed him. His Stah sensed that their father was home and knew exactly what they were up to, so he and his brother ran home as fast as they could.

When they arrived back at the camp, the father said to them, "I warned you, my sons. Those birds could have killed you."

His Stah replied, "Yes, they are mean. They killed my brother many times. He is not strong, but I brought him back every time."

The father shook his head and said, "I have warned you against many things. You defy me and do what I have told you not to do." He was now assured that his suspicions were correct about His Stah. He was indeed a powerful medicine man.

"Shadow," said Nam Shim, "this is the end of the story about how His Stah came into being, and from this time on, His Stah had many more adventures."

Shadow was intrigued with every story Nam Shim told her. Soon the nights were filled with stories, and Old Nam Shim's audience grew larger. Other children, as well as adults, soon began sitting around the fire outside his home. Even though his audience grew in numbers, Old Nam Shim still directed his stories towards the one he called Shadow.

*Now, Shadow, I will tell this story the way I heard it. Red Hollow Log
is the name of the little boy that I will talk about.*

Once, the Tse Tse Stus were all camping. There was an old
woman who was unwanted. She was poor, and nobody would have anything to do with her.

One day she went into the forest to gather wood. As she did, she
heard a baby cry and looked for it. The old woman soon found the baby lying
in a rotten, hollow log. The old woman picked up the baby and was happy to
see him. She said, "Someone was very nice to me. Someone felt sorry for me.
Now I will have someone to take care of me and do things for me. It was very
nice of the person who gave me this child." She wrapped the baby in her
blanket and took him home. When she got home, she cleaned him up.

The old woman made tea out of wild rosebush roots. The baby
grew up on this tea. As the days went by, the baby learned fast and grew
up fast. This was unusual, for it was a time of great hunger. On the fourth
day of the fourth week that he was with the old woman, he grew quite a
bit more, and on that day the boy said to his grandmother (the old
woman), "Make me a bow and some arrows."

The old woman made a bow and arrows and gave them to him,
and he said, "Make me a ball." She did this and gave it to him. He said,
"Tomorrow morning, before the sun comes up, you must go up the hill. I
will be on the other side of the hill, sitting. You must roll the ball down
the hill. Then you must say, 'Shoot this that is coming down the hill. You
shoot this, Red Hollow Log, that is coming down.' "

The old woman did everything that her grandson ordered her to
do. She rolled the ball down and said, "You shoot this that is coming down
the hill, Red Hollow Log." He shot the ball, and there lay a buffalo
(ésevone).

"Now you skin it," said Red Hollow Log, and the old woman
butchered it. After she had butchered it, she took the meat home and
made dried meat. The meat was thoroughly dry, but this buffalo had a lot
of fat on it. Red Hollow Log told his grandmother this: "That man who
is the chief has two daughters, one who is single and one who is married
to a very handsome man. Both daughters are beautiful." He also told his
grandmother this: "You go to that chief's home and take this fat." Just
before you leave, drop the fat and then pick it up and say, 'Oh, I dropped
my grandson's ointment for his eyes.' "

So she went to the chief's home. The people had seen her with a
little boy before, when she had been poor and was asking for food. People
remembered the boy as being nasty—he was dirty and always had sleep

in his eyes. The village and the chief's daughters remembered him as being ugly. The old woman went to the house of the chief and walked in. Just before she left, she dropped the fat, picked it up, and said, "Oh, I accidentally dropped my grandson's ointment for his eyes."

Everyone was hungry. The girl who was single saw the fat. "Wait, old woman. Hand me that fat, and let me eat it." She grabbed the fat and ate it.

"I was just carrying my grandson's eye ointment." The old lady walked out and returned to her home.

When she got back, Red Hollow Log asked her, even though he already knew, "What did they do?"

She told him what had happened. She said, "The unmarried girl really wanted to eat it, and I left it for her."

"Grandmother, I want you to go back again tomorrow and tell the chief, 'My grandson, Red Hollow Log, sent me over to ask you if he can marry your daughter.' Tell him that I will bring dry meat."

The next day, the old woman went to the chief's lodge again. She walked in and told him, "The reason I came is that my grandson, Red Hollow Log, wants to marry your daughter. What do you say? If you say 'yes,' I will bring the dried meat."

The chief said, "Yes, you bring the dried meat."

Lodge liner

Stories of Magic and Medicine Men

After the chief had agreed, the married daughter said, interrupting her father, "I don't want her to marry that filthy, dirty boy. He always has sleep in his eyes. His hair is always tangled. He is so ugly!"

The chief said to the old woman, "Don't pay any attention to what she said. Go ahead and bring the dried meat tomorrow, and I will have a lodge put up. Then your grandson can come home and be my son-in-law."

"Yes," the old woman said, "I will bring the dried meat right away."

The chief said, "He will marry my daughter tomorrow."

The old woman took the dried meat to the chief the next day, and everybody was so happy to have dried meat to eat, because everyone was starving. The lodge was up, and Red Hollow Log went to it. The chief said to some people, "Bring the old woman's lodge and things over to where I am camping." The old woman would now be cared for.

Red Hollow Log married the girl. She was beautiful, and he was still ugly. But the next day, when they walked into the chief's lodge, miraculously, Red Hollow Log was now handsome, better-looking than any person in the village—even the older daughter's husband, his brother-in-law. Everyone in the lodge was afraid and shy and would not look at Red Hollow Log, especially his sister-in-law, because she hated him.

The next day, the older daughter was sitting with her husband by the door. As Red Hollow Log was walking out, he put his hand on her shoulder. His hand left a mark on her shoulder. The mark was the color of a yellow-brown powder used for body paint. Now that Red Hollow Log was no longer ugly, the girl bragged to everyone, saying, "This is where Red Hollow Log put his hand on me."

Red Hollow Log and his wife often went for walks. One day, they were going over a ridge and everyone in the village watched them, for they were highly admired for their good looks. As they walked, red birds flew about their shoulders and heads.

One day they went over the hill. Red Hollow Log told his wife to gather buffalo chips and put them in a row at the bottom of the hill. The girl did what her husband told her, and they returned to the village. He told his wife to tell the chief, her father, to go hunting for buffalo the next day before sunrise. The chief, also being a village crier, was to announce the night before that the buffalo were just over the hill. The girl told this to her father. He announced to the people that buffalo had been given to them, that there were many just over the hill, and that everyone who wanted to hunt could go hunting. All the young men were ready at dawn, and they all left to hunt. The village had no meat, and people were hungry.

When the men went over the hill, they saw 40 buffalo. The men killed every buffalo, and they dressed the meat. They had meat to last for quite a while.

The older sister's husband envied Red Hollow Log for all the things he had done to help the people. One day the husband said to his wife, "Let's walk up to the hill where Red Hollow Log and his wife went." He caught a red bird and tied it with a buckskin thong to his wife's shoulder to make it appear as though the bird was attracted to them. Everyone watched them as they walked up the hill. He had heard what Red Hollow Log had done with the buffalo chips. He told his wife to gather buffalo chips and place them just as Red Hollow Log's wife had done. When they got back to the village, he told his wife to have her father, the chief, announce that there would be buffalo over the hill. The next day the hunters went out but found no buffalo. The hunters returned empty-handed, but they had found the buffalo chips.

Red Hollow Log told his brother- and sister-in-law to move in with him and his wife, into their lodge. They did this. At night, the brother-in-law saw that while Red Hollow Log and his wife slept, their quilts glowed and sparkled blue. The brother-in-law wanted his blankets to glow. So he built a fire and prepared hot coals. He placed these coals on his blankets. The buffalo robes (blankets), of course, were singed and shriveled. His wife was angry with him. She said, "What did you do that for? You ruined our robes, and now it is smoky in this lodge." They threw their robes outside. When the chief heard of this, he told his oldest daughter to tell her husband to go away because he made a fool of himself and his family. The chief also said that her husband would never be able to do the things that Red Hollow Log had done because Red Hollow Log was a medicine man.

Red Hollow Log then married the older sister and had two wives. One morning, when they awoke, the older sister looked exactly like her younger sister. Everyone in the village admired all three of them as they walked about. It is said that the whole village became more prosperous, and everyone was happy.

O̦ne night when it was quiet and clear, when the whole universe seemed visible, Shadow lay on her back beside Nam Shim, staring at the stars. "Sometimes, Nam Shim, I wish that I could be up there playing among the stars. Don't you think that would be fun? Which one would you choose for your own?"

"I don't know, Little One. Sometimes you have to be careful what you wish for. Once, a long time ago, my two sisters were fighting over who would get the brightest star in the heavens. To stop their quarreling, my mother told them the story of a baby called Star."

She told them that once there were two girls who were very good friends. One night they were lying on their backs looking at the stars. "That bright star, I wish it were my boyfriend," said one.

"I will choose that one," said the other girl, pointing to a dimmer star.

They went to bed, and the next morning when they awoke, they were among the stars. The bright star was a very old man with white hair. The old man spoke to the girl, "You chose me, so now I am taking you. You are mine." The dimmer star was a young and handsome man. He spoke to the girl who had chosen him, saying the same thing that the old one had said.

The two stars took the girls who had chosen them and went in different directions. The stars married the girls. The girl married to the young man became pregnant. As the time grew near for her to give birth to her child, the girls visited each other. The girl who was married to the old man was lonesome and said to her friend, "I wonder how we could escape to go back to our people."

The other girl said that she knew of a way. "We will weave a rope from the reeds growing by the Milky Way. When our husbands are away hunting, we will wet the end and lower it to the ground. If it is muddy when we pull it up, we will know that it is long enough. If not, we will make it longer."

When the husbands went hunting, the two girls gathered reeds and wove the rope. For days and days they worked. Each day, they wet the rope and lowered it. For days and days more they worked. Each day, they wet the rope and lowered it. Each night they hid the rope near the Milky Way.

One day when they pulled up the rope, it had mud on it. They were happy because they knew that the rope, finally, was long enough.

The next morning, the girl who was pregnant said, "I will go down first." Unknown to the girls was the fact that the previous day the rope had hit the top of a mountain, and when the pregnant girl reached the end of the rope, she found that it was not long enough. She tried to climb back up but fell. The fall didn't kill her, but she gave birth to her baby, and it was not stillborn. Not knowing what had happened, the other girl climbed down but also fell.

The baby was a little boy, and he was known as Star.

Shadow had loved the stories of magic and medicine men, but she had loved even more the stories Old Nam Shim told about himself and the people he knew. She longed to hear those stories once again from the lips of the old man himself, but like those he had spoken of in his stories, Nam Shim, too, was now gone. But he had instilled a pride in her that no one could ever take away, and it had happened one day when she was only 12 years old.

As the day began its journey into night, the old man could hear the boys teasing and taunting Shadow as they played outside.

"You can't be a warrior, you're a girl! Everyone knows girls weren't warriors. Come, Shadow, and pretend you are cooking for us!" they laughed. It was then that their laughter was cut short by Nam Shim's voice.

"Whoa, boys! What's this I hear you say? There were no warriors who were women? Come sit by my side, and I will correct what you have said. Many Tse Tse Stus women became great warriors. I myself knew two personally. One was called Buffalo Calf Road Woman—she fought against Custer at the Little Big Horn. She fought so bravely that Crazy Horse, the great Lakota war leader, once honored her. The other warrior I knew, and fought alongside for many years, was Mochi."

Discussion and Activities

Goals

- Recount the Cheyenne stories that were traditional to their culture.

- Understand the importance of keeping cultural stories alive.

Discussion Questions

1. In most stories, there is a lesson to be taught. The story of the girl-horse has two lessons. What are they?

    Answer: Certainly the girl had to pay a price for disobeying her parents, but she also took responsibility for her actions.

2. What does His Stah mean? Why was he called this?

    Answer: "Belly button." He was created from the placenta of a boy.

3. His Stah was a powerful medicine man. What events in the story proved this point to the father?

    Answer: His Stah put the rattles of snakes inside his and his brother's heads. His Stah could bring his brother back to life each time he died.

4. How did Red Hollow Log get his name?

    Answer: He was found in a hollow log by the old woman who raised him.

5. What magical feats did Red Hollow Log perform?

    Answer: He turned a ball into a buffalo. He transformed himself into a handsome young man. He brought buffalo herds near the tribe so they could hunt, thus making the whole village prosperous.

6. What was the magic performed in the story about Star?

    Answer: The girls made a wish about two stars, and their wishes came true.

Things to Do

Class Discussion

Define *culture* (the development of the intellect through education and training) for the students. Discuss such elements as customs, celebrations, literature, education, housing, food, clothing, language, and economies—all the things that make a culture unique. Also discuss the elements that are common to all cultures: a belief system, language and customs, religion, clothing, and social behavior. Building on this discussion, begin a brainstorming chart comparing the Cheyenne culture and the white man's culture. (Students will use this chart in the library research activity below.)

Literature

One of the common threads among cultures is storytelling, especially stories that teach lessons, such as the ones in this chapter. Find other examples of stories with lessons to share with students. *Aesop's Fables* are a good example, and most students will be familiar with these stories. Discuss the similarities and differences among these stories. Students may want to share stories that they have heard in their families.

Writing/Art Activity

Have students write their own fables, stories that teach a lesson. Have students illustrate their stories and share them with the class.

Library Research

Building on the discussion of culture (above), have students choose and research another culture that interests them. Have the class add these cultures to their comparison chart.

Class Bulletin Board

Add the culture comparison chart developed in the classroom discussion and library research activities.

Put students' written fables in a book for display.

6

History and Heroes

Mochi

I would say that she was one of the fiercest warriors of the Bow String Society. I knew Mochi[1] (Mo ke, or Mó'kė̃huduovse) from the time we were camped at Póénẽõ ó'he'e, the Tse Tse Stus word that means Dry Creek, the place the whites called Sand Creek. She was the only one of our women, and the only Native American woman in America, who was ever sent to prison as a prisoner of war.

The story of her birth is as old as the Tse Tse Stus, for there were many things that needed to be done before a child could be brought into this world. Mochi was born in 1841, in the land of the Yellowstone (Wyoming) to parents whose names have been forgotten in time.

When Mochi's mother (náhko'e) knew she was with child, she immediately took measures to ensure that she and her unborn baby would be healthy. She and her people believed that babies grew early in the morning, and that exercising helped the unborn baby grow. Each day she awoke before the people in her camp to take long morning walks.

During Mochi's mother's time of pregnancy, her husband helped her by carrying the water and wood for the lodge, even though his main duties included hunting, making war articles, and making drums. Mochi's mother learned many important things from her elders during that time. They told her she must not stare at anything too long, for they believed it would mark her unborn baby for life.

When her time to give birth finally arrived, Mochi's mother walked to a small lodge specially built for this occasion. At the center of the lodge, a pole was firmly planted in the ground in an upright position. She grasped this pole as she knelt on a robe cushioned by a thick layer of grass. Encouraged by the medicine man's songs and rattle, and accompanied by older, experienced female relatives, Mochi's mother strained to give her birth.

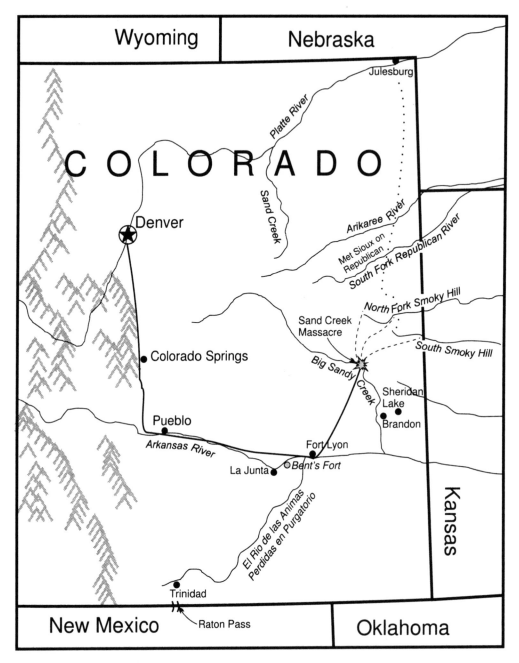

Wyoming

Nebraska

COLORADO

Platte River

Julesburg

Sand Creek

Denver

Arikaree River

Met Sioux on
Republican

South Fork Republican River

North Fork Smoky Hill

Sand Creek
Massacre

South Smoky Hill

Colorado Springs

Big Sandy Creek

Sheridan
Lake

Brandon

Pueblo

Arkansas River

Fort Lyon

La Junta

Bent's Fort

Kansas

El Rio de las Animas
Perdidas en Purgatorio

Trinidad

New Mexico

Raton Pass

Oklahoma

———— Chivington's March, 1864

- - - - - - Cheyenne Escape, 1864

··········· Sioux and Cheyenne Route
to Julesburg, January 1865

⊙ Indicates a fort

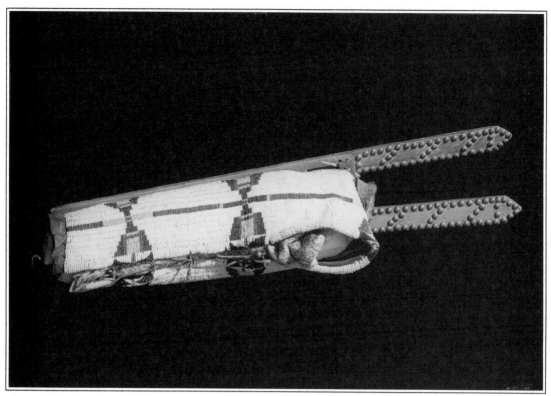

Cradleboard

As soon as Mochi arrived into this world, the midwives immediately greased and powdered her body with finely ground, dried manure and decayed cottonwood pulp to protect her from evil. The midwives tickled Mochi's mother's throat to help her expel the placenta, which was then placed in a deerskin bag. Her people believed that if they buried the placenta, the baby would die, so the bag was tied to a tree. The midwives rubbed dried spores of star puffball fungus on Mochi's umbilical cord until it fell away from her body. The women cut the cord in two and wrapped one half in a soft piece of beaded buckskin, which was then shaped into a pouch and sewn together. Mochi's grandmother (néške'e) beaded the other half of the umbilical cord and placed it inside her cradle to ensure long life and protection from evil spirits. She placed a piece of beaded umbilical cord of an animal on the outside of the cradle to fool any evil spirits that might come visiting. A design was beaded onto a deer-skin pouch, which contained the baby's umbilical cord.

The design represented either the lizard or the turtle. To the Tse Tse Stus, the lizard symbolized stamina. It was known to endure long periods of heat without water and could survive in the harshest of environments. To the Tse Tse Stus, the turtle represented a strong heart, for they had seen its heart beat after its head had been cut off. When Mochi's father (ného'e) saw that all had gone well in his daughter's birth, he rushed from his lodge and gave a great yell while firing his musket into the air. This proud father knew what would have to be accomplished during his daughter's first year of life if she were to survive.

Cradleboard covering

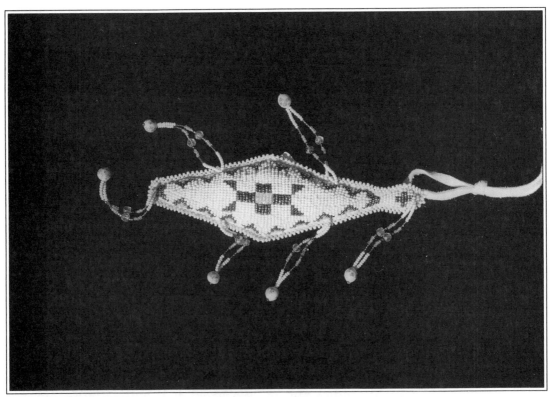

Umbilical pouch

The naming of a child, though, came from her paternal elders. It is not known whether her paternal grandmother or aunt (nåháa'e) performed the naming ceremony. In either case, she was blessed by her elders, lovingly and reverently. These relatives talked to her parents of the old ways of the Tse Tse Stus. They said that if any trouble or disagreement should arise between the mother and father, they should not involve the child, for she was a gift from Maheo, the Creator. The elder again blessed the child, and named her Mochi (Buffalo Calf Woman). Tse Tse Stus customs use animal names or physical traits in naming their children.

When Mochi reached three weeks of age, her grandmother completed construction of her first cradle. She beaded a soft deerskin around the wooden frame. She also wove a soft skin inside the frame so her grandchild could be securely strapped and lie comfortably in the cradle. The cradle's construction offered great versatility for the mother's everyday chores. It could either be strapped on her back or hung in a tree. Mochi's grandmother also placed two sharpened branches, each about an inch in diameter and 18 inches long, on each side of the cradle to protect her grandchild from injury if she accidentally fell from her mother's horse. She believed that the sharpened points would cause the cradle to stick in the ground. The sharpened poles conveniently stabilized the cradle when it was propped against a solid object. Mochi's grandmother taught these skills to all of her female children (ka'ĕko'neho). She also taught them the importance of quickly and quietly removing a crying infant from campsites because of the risk of giving away the camp's location to enemy scouts.

For the first five years of Mochi's life, her parents allowed her to be a typical child. She filled her days playing games with dolls and small tipis she constructed with sticks and pieces of deerskin. She never lacked for love or attention, and her mother continued to nurse her during these years. Her parents also allowed her, within safety's measure, to explore her natural curiosity. During this time, her mother taught her to help with the simple chores of carrying kindling wood and small bags of water. By the end of Mochi's fifth year, her mother had begun teaching her the traditional chores of young Tse Tse Stus girls.

Like you are doing now, Shadow, she and other youngsters sat around the village campfires and listened to the old ones tell the stories of their history, customs, and religion. The old ones taught them, as I have tried to teach you, to be generous, kind, and helpful to others, so as not to be talked about by other tribal members. Mochi's life followed this path until she reached her ninth year, when she was no longer allowed to play games with boys and started doing the work for which she had been trained: skinning, tanning hides, sewing, beading, and cooking. When she reached puberty, another great ceremony was held in her honor. Her father, upon learning she had just experienced her first menstrual cycle, proudly and loudly let the rest of the village know his daughter was now a woman. Those wishing to marry her might begin the ritual courtship.

In the old days, a young man who wished to marry her would have to bring many presents on horses to Mochi's father. This was not an attempt to "buy" her but was merely to show the father that the young man would be a great provider for his daughter. This was important, for fathers then, as today, cared deeply for their daughters and wanted them to marry a good man. Now, if he were accepted by the father, the young man would never be left alone with the daughter. This is something our customs forbade. The ritual required the young woman to be always accompanied by a girlfriend or sister. On the wedding day, as the only ceremony, there would be blessings and prayers by a holy man.

A young man did court Mochi, and they were married. The night of Mochi's marriage, the groom's best friend carried Mochi into the wedding lodge. She was dressed in the clothing her husband had brought her, and his other gifts covered her arms and neck. Mochi also brought her protective rope. She wore this braided rope, which encircled her waist beneath her clothing and was wound around her thighs down to her knees. This rope was worn for the first few nights of a marriage so that the husband and wife could truly get to know each other, without being blinded by their passions. The rope was to be respected by the groom as long as the bride decided to wear it.

From her time of marriage to the time of the Sand Creek Massacre, Mochi lived in much the same way as her parents had. Colonel John Chivington, though, altered her lifestyle on that infamous November day in 1864. His actions caused the loss of many Tse Tse Stus lives, but the memories of those who died in the Sand Creek Massacre live on. Such was the case of Mochi's first husband. His name was White Shield, and he died defending Mochi's lodge. What is known of her actions was told after the massacre. Her story on that day was interwoven with all those who were there. So her story must be told, in turn, in the tale of the Sand Creek Massacre.

Umbilical pouch

During the summer of 1864, before the massacre at Sand Creek, Major Wynkoop escorted Black Kettle and other Cheyenne chiefs to a meeting with Governor Evans at Camp Weld (just outside of Denver). Photograph courtesy Colorado Historical Society

"Nam Shim, what caused the white man to do what he did in the time of the Sand Creek Massacre?" asked Shadow.

Little One, not all whites of the time were evil. I remember men like William Bent, who not only tried to keep the peace but also married into our tribe. When his first wife, Owl Woman, died in childbirth, he followed Cheyenne custom and married her sister, Yellow Woman.

And there was the one we call Tall Chief (Major Edward) Wynkoop. He tried hard to keep the peace after he met Chief One Eye and, later, Black Kettle (Mó'ȯhtávetoo'o). He was the one who, along with another man named Silas Soule, brought Black Kettle and the other chiefs to Denver to make peace with Governor Evans and Colonel Chivington. These were good men. It was Colonel Chivington, though, who created the problems that led to the wars. This colonel was, at one time, a holy man of the white man's God. Having known him is one of the reasons I have never embraced the white man's religion. I have never understood how men who believed in a God of love could so easily kill others who did not share their beliefs.

Anyway, Shadow, from the time of the mass migration of whites into our land, we had skirmishes with the ve hoes (white men). Many of these people came west hearing that we were all savages. They shot at us only because we were Tse Tse Stus. Many of our warriors shot back. Violence begot more violence. Our great chief, Lean Bear, after personally meeting with the Great White Father Lincoln and promising to keep the peace, was murdered by Lieutenant Eayres as he was trying to show him the medal Lincoln had given him. Just after this encounter, the Hungate family was killed outside Denver by revenge-seeking Arapaho warriors. The people of Denver put the bodies of Ward Hungate, his wife, and two children on public display. This hardened the hearts of all who saw them. It was what Colonel Chivington wanted. No peace would be found as long as Colonel Chivington was around. His heart was cold to us. He made sure there would be no peace without bloodshed by getting rid of Tall Chief Wynkoop. Chivington removed our friend from command of Fort Lyon because Tall Chief Wynkoop was trying hard to make peace between the two cultures. Chivington replaced him with a man we all hated. His name was Major Scott Anthony.

Black Kettle   Photograph courtesy Colorado Historical Society

Colonel Chivington's first step was for Anthony, as new commander of Fort Lyon, to banish all Cheyenne and Arapaho from U.S. government property. Anthony informed Black Kettle and the others they would be safe if they camped near Sand Creek and flew an American flag over their village. Anthony also told the chiefs to send their warriors out to hunt, because winter was fast approaching.

On November 26, the interpreter John Smith, Private David Louderback, and a teamster headed for our village at Sand Creek with a wagonload of trade goods. George Bent and his half brother, Charlie, who were the sons of Owl Woman and Yellow Woman, and Little White Man (Vé'ho'kĕso, or Stay ah veho)—our name for William Bent—were in the village visiting their mothers' people.

On November 28, 1864, two days after Wynkoop's departure from Fort Lyon, Tall Chief Wynkoop encountered No-ta-nee, an Arapaho warrior he knew. Black Kettle chose No-ta-nee and two other warriors to alert Wynkoop that a war party of 200 Sioux was in the area, and that he should beware.

That evening, an army of 700 men, commanded by the giant Colonel Chivington, who was riding a large mule, stole their way through the darkness of November's star-chilled night. Just before the first light and dawn, these men in blue stood on a knoll west of our village. There they waited, like a dark shroud ready to cover the frosty morning's light.

I remember that morning quite well—it was not unlike other autumn mornings on Colorado's eastern plains. The darkened sky had not yet yielded to the sun, and night's chill still held morning's air in her grasp. Smoke rising from village fires seemed to reach up in silent praise to herald this dawn's arrival. All was still on Sand Creek's banks on that frost-covered morning of November 29, 1864.

There were at least five Cheyenne bands and 10 lodges of Left Hand's Arapaho camped there for the winter. Though most of the village's warriors had gone buffalo hunting for winter's food supply, there remained a sense of security at Sand Creek. Black Kettle's people were told that their safety against attack by the army, or by any white intruders, was ensured as long as a large garrison-sized American flag (six foot by twelve foot) flew over their village. The stillness quieting this November morning was much like the calm before a storm, but the violence following the tranquility and beauty of this day forever changed the ways of our people and of the Arapaho.

To those who observed the beauty of November's dawn, it offered a quiet respite from the drudgery of everyday work. Yet no eloquence was spoken of the women's morning duties. Their day began before first light as they gathered firewood to keep the night's fire burning warm into the morning to cook breakfast for their families. Infants and small children were cared for as their needs required. Youngsters old enough to help were given daily tasks. Those responsibilities were fulfilled, regardless of weather, for the welfare of the Tse Tse Stus.

Though our families and village were of utmost importance, our hospitality to visitors was famous. On the morning of Chivington's attack, there were white visitors in our midst—Private David Louderback, trader John Smith and his son Jack, and a teamster named Clark. They had arrived only two days earlier to promote trade with the "friendlies" in the area.

On their third day in the village, Louderback and others awoke to a pleasant morning, but they heard a sound coming from over the horizon. It was ever so soft at first, as though the wind's rhythm with mother earth had broken the serenity of autumn's morn. The village dogs heard it—the horses, too. The distant sounds of pounding hooves echoed through the village like a rolling clap of thunder. Some of the women and children thought that the rumbling noise was a herd of buffalo, but Yellow Wolf and the other old ones knew the sound to be something else: horses—white men's horses. Private David Louderback was enjoying breakfast in his lodge when a Cheyenne woman entered and said that a herd of buffalo were coming. Moments later, a chief entered and told the

Yellow Wolf (Heóve'hó'nehe), about age 50; age information from Marella Panana, great-great-granddaughter of Yellow Wolf

Photograph courtesy Colorado Historical Society

private that there were many soldiers approaching the village. Louderback immediately left his lodge to investigate the commotion stirring in the village. What he witnessed caused his blood to run cold. There on a hill, poised to strike, were Chivington's troops. He hastened Jack Smith to get him a horse, but none were available. The women had already taken the village's small pony herd to a safe place. The presence of those soldiers represented a threat to one of the tribe's most prized possessions—horses.

Thinking that our horses were safe, our people now came out of their lodges as the rumbling noise came closer. Black Kettle and White Antelope saw the gathering troops on a knoll west of the village, and they urged our people not to panic or run. The chiefs beckoned all of us to the village's center, where the American flag was unfurled. Black Kettle called for his people to remain calm, reminding them that the flag protected their camp: There was no danger. Our people were unaware that Death had come to them this day, and he had come to the Cheyenne and Arapaho as a vile, perverted visitor.

With his troops poised for action, Colonel Chivington ordered his artillery to set up. He methodically rode amongst his troops urging them to "remember our wives and children murdered on the Platte and Arkansas." At one point, old Jim Beckwourth, the black-white man, told me he had heard Chivington say, "I don't tell you to kill all ages and sex, but look back on the plains of the Platte, where your mothers, fathers, brothers, and sisters have been slain, and their blood saturating the sands on the Platte." The orders by Colonel Chivington and Colonel Shoup were simple: There were to be no prisoners! On that cold November day, between the first light and dawn, the bugles sounded "attack." Morning's fragile veil was forever torn when Chivington's artillery rained down its carnage upon our village.

With the first sounds of battle, George and Charlie Bent ran from their lodge, as did I. We were astonished to find the village under attack. As we came out into the open, we discovered most of the village in panic. People of all ages ran, not knowing where to go or which way to turn.

Charlie Bent stayed in camp to see if the attack would cease. It did not. Charlie and John Smith's son, Jack, later surrendered to Jim Beckwourth and soldiers they knew. They came to regret their decision.

Meanwhile, I watched George Bent race back to his lodge and retrieve his weapons. Armed, he ran west towards the protection of the sand hills. When he arrived there, he found a group of middle-aged Cheyenne men. They organized what little firepower they possessed and made a brief stand at this location until a cavalry troop overran their position. Fleeing from this new threat, they jumped into a dry streambed above the Cheyenne camps. Before they reached safety, however, they ran headlong into another company of cavalry, who opened fire on Bent and the others as they rode up on the opposite bank of the stream. Faced with a company of cavalry on either side of us, we Tse Tse Stus had one choice—run for our lives through the streambed's deadly gauntlet of gunfire.

Many people, including myself, had preceded George Bent's race for life. What my people and I witnessed on our run was horrible—old men, women, and children "lying thickly scattered on the sand, some dead, and the rest too badly wounded to move," as though the Third Colorado Volunteers were a nightmare come true. They relentlessly pursued us. November's frost-laden air burned our lungs with each breath we took as we ran for two miles. After racing around an obstacle course of the dead and dying, we finally reached a place where the river banks were high and steep. Exhausted, we stopped and found a large group of Cheyenne who had also sought shelter there. Older men and women hastily dug pits and holes into the frozen ground. Like giant prairie dogs, they burrowed for protection into those banks.

While looking at these earth works, a force hit George Bent and knocked him face-first into the earth. He told me the sand in his mouth tasted cold and bitter as his mind tried to comprehend what had happened to his body. Soon a warm liquid covered his lower limbs as a hot searing pain scorched his very being. Realizing that he had been shot through his hip culminated the day's madness in his mind. He struggled and then managed to tumble into one of the holes, already filled with men, women, and children. The day's freezing temperatures did one good thing for George Bent: It froze the blood from his wounds and kept him from bleeding to death.

As the wounded Bent and the rest of us took cover in the holes, Chivington's troops surrounded our position. Worked into a killing frenzy, the soldiers poured murderous fire into our besieged shelter. Fortunately, the holes offered more than enough protection. The troops stayed there until darkness again covered the day. Under night's cover, our band of half-naked survivors escaped and fled north.

The madness didn't stop with just our people. I later heard that, earlier, Private David Louderback, dressed in his uniform shirt, trousers, and socks, fastened a white handkerchief to a stick. While he held his flag of truce high, Louderback and John Smith, dressed in civilian clothes, approached Chivington's troops. When they were about 150 yards from the soldiers, members of Colorado's Third opened fire on them. Like the Cheyenne and Arapaho around them, Louderback and Smith were now under attack. As they too ran for their lives, dodging bullets and shell bursts, Smith heard some of the soldiers yell at one another, "Shoot that old bastard!" Louderback and Smith found temporary shelter in the same lodge in which they'd spent the night.

Louderback, protected only by lodge skins, kept looking out the entrance, watching for Colonel Chivington. He later testified, "I saw him crossing the creek, at the lower end of the village. I watched him until he came up within 40 or 50 yards of the lodge, and I hollered to him, calling him by name, and he told me to come on, that I was all right, calling me by name. I went out to him, and in going out a man fired at me. I asked the Colonel what they were firing at me for, and he turned around and told them to stop firing. He then told me to fall in the rear of the command, that I was all right. I told him to hold on a minute, the lodge was full of white men, pointing a lodge out to him in which John Smith was." Smith; his son, Jack; Charlie Bent; Clark; and Louderback were temporarily out of harm's way.

Black Kettle could not believe what was happening. He, too, made a white flag of truce and hoisted it on his flagpole, beneath "Old Glory." Chivington's men ignored the chief's gesture and charged down upon him. Black Kettle grabbed his wife, Medicine Calf, and they ran for their lives. They, too, followed the same creek bed through the same gauntlet that the others and I had barely survived. After a short while, Medicine Calf stopped and fell limp. She had been shot by the soldiers. Black Kettle saw that she did not move as the sickening "thud" sounds made by their bullets continued to hit her body. He wanted to stop but knew any pause in his flight meant death. He continued his run up the creek to where his people hid in the pits.

When night came, Black Kettle crept out to where his wife had fallen. After thoroughly searching through the dead and dying, he found her—alive! Although shot nine times, Medicine Calf clung tenuously to life. Black Kettle carried her back to safety. Then he and Medicine Calf also vanished from Chivington's troops under the cover of darkness to seek help.

Shadow, we lost so many of our greatest people on that terrible day. When that morning first exploded into gunfire, one of our chiefs, 75-year-old White Antelope, emerged from his lodge with his arms raised and shouted in English, "Stop, stop!" Still the carnage continued. When he realized that it was hopeless, he stood tall and folded his arms and began to sing the Cheyenne Death Song: Nothing lives long, only the earth and mountains. They shot him down. I watched as a trooper dismounted from his horse and mutilated the old man's body with a knife.

He scalped White Antelope. He also cut off White Antelope's nose, ears, and private parts and bragged that he was going to make a new tobacco pouch from the freshly severed parts of the old chief.

I saw Robert Bent upon the knoll with Chivington's men. He, the oldest son of Owl Woman and William Bent, had been taken prisoner by Chivington and forced to guide the soldiers to our village. Robert later told me he heard the screams of women and children. He watched helplessly as his mother's people were butchered. During the carnage, he witnessed five women hiding under a bank. When the soldiers came up to them, the women showed themselves and begged for mercy, but the troopers shot them all. On another bank, one woman was lying on the ground with a broken leg. A soldier came up to her with his long knife poised. She raised her arm to protect herself as he struck her. The blow broke her arm. She rolled over and raised her other arm as he struck her again, breaking her other arm, and then left her there without killing her. Robert also told me that he witnessed a group of about 40 women run to a gully for protection. When the soldiers approached, the women sent a young six-year-old girl out with a white flag. He remembered the sight of this child as she was shot in the head by a soldier. The others were also killed. He watched in silent rage as soldiers raped, scalped, and mutilated the women—one young mother was found with her unborn child cut out and lying beside her.

It was during this time that the saga of 24-year-old Mochi began. As the atrocities of that day continued, Mochi's husband put her in their lodge along with her mother. He and her father then attempted to fight off the oncoming soldiers. Outnumbered and outgunned, they stood no chance against Chivington's horde of soldiers, and Mochi knew that death lurked just outside her lodge's door. She heard her father and husband's death cries just before a soldier entered their lodge. As the soldier came in, he immediately shot Mochi's mother in the head. Then he turned his attention towards the tall, beautiful woman. She could see it in his eyes: Before he killed her, he would rape her. The large man in blue grabbed Mochi and tried to throw her to the ground, but she broke free of his grasp. She knew she must fight or die. As he lunged towards her again, she evaded his hands and scurried to where her grandfather's buffalo gun lay in the lodge. This was the same gun given to her grandfather five years before by two white gold-seekers. Her grandfather had saved them from starvation on the Smoky Hill Trail. Grabbing the gun, she turned and fired towards the man in blue. He died without knowing how his death had come. All seemed still inside the lodge as tragedy and chaos broke loose outside. Half in shock and half enraged, Mochi fled her lodge and ran towards the north, seeking cover. Following a trail marked by the dead and wounded Tse Tse Stus, Mochi found the remnants of her people who had dug into late autumn's frozen ground, seeking cover from the army's murderous fire. Mochi realized as she joined their frantic dig that she would no longer perform the duties of the traditional Tse Tse Stus woman. She would put aside all her life's lessons to become a warrior.

On that November morning, the month of the Hard-Face Moon, Mochi was reborn a Tse Tse Stus warrior. For the next 11 years, this 130-pound woman, who stood 5 feet 6¾ inches, lived both a warrior's and a mother's life.

Old Yellow Wolf was 85 years old on this last day of his life. The November morning brought horrible deaths for him and half of his Hair Rope Men (Heévåhetaneo'o, the term used by Northern Tse Tse Stus for their southern brethen). The soldiers mutilated Old Yellow Wolf much the same way they had butchered White Antelope. He knew that The Wise One Above would greet many of his children's spirits rising from Sand Creek's frost-laden ground.

Before the morning's attack, my friend Little Bear had awakened early and left his lodge to find the pony herd's location. His brother-in-law, Tomahawk, had hidden the herd the night before as a safety precaution against Cheyenne enemies. As he approached the area where the horses were supposed to be, he found that they were gone. As he searched for them, another Cheyenne, Kingfisher, surprised Little Bear by the speed with which he ran towards him. Breathlessly, Kingfisher told him that white soldiers had just run off their herd.

After hearing this, Little Bear ran to a lookout point that surveyed the Fort Lyon Trail to look for signs of the missing herd. He soon knew what had happened. He was amazed to see soldiers leaving with the herd. He and Kingfisher ran as fast as they could back to their village, already under attack. Dodging bullets and cannon fire, Little Bear raced to his lodge and grabbed his bow, his quiver of arrows, and his war bonnet and shield. The thick of the battle now surrounded him. With his weapons in hand, he, too, headed for the streambed so many before had followed. He, too, saw the dead and wounded as he ran through the troops' deadly hail of fire. The shooting was so intense by the time Little Bear reached the pit's safety that all the feathers in his war bonnet had been shot out. Miraculously, he was unharmed.

When the fighting had subsided, Little Bear and I searched the creek bed for survivors. What we found made our mouths go dry. Then, like a summer storm's flash flood, rage and hatred surged in us, drowning out all of our other emotions. Revenge consumed our thoughts, leaving no room for compassion. All the dead had been mutilated. Even the wounded had been scalped. We found an old women wandering about— her entire scalp had been taken off, and the blood was running down into her eyes so that she could not see where to go.

The magnitude of this carnage sickened many of the soldiers and scouts at Sand Creek, who later testified in military and congressional hearings. What followed made First Lieutenant James Olney of the First Colorado Cavalry nauseous and disgusted. He later said at the white man's hearing about the massacre that he observed three women and five children, who were prisoners in the charge of some soldiers; that, while being conducted along, they were approached by Lieutenant Harry Richmond, of the Third Colorado Cavalry; that Lieutenant Richmond thereupon immediately killed and scalped the three women and the five children while they [the prisoners] were screaming for mercy. . . ." Early in the slaughter, Captain Silas Soule ordered his men *not* to fire on any of the Cheyenne. Towards the massacre's frenzied peak, he positioned his men between Chivington's troops and the fleeing Cheyenne, so that the Indians could not be fired on. For this act of defiance, Chivington never forgave Soule.

Like devils born from Hell, the Third Colorado Cavalry, commanded by Colonel George L. Shoup, commenced the wholesale slaughter and mutilation of men, women, and children. They severed women's breasts and made them into scurrilous trophies. The pubic areas of females of all ages were cut out as a gruesome reminder of what Chivington once said about our children: "Nits grow into lice." The shooting lasted for about eight hours, but the carnage continued into the night. Chivington's troops killed about 137 of our people and of the Arapaho— 98 of the dead were women and children—but Death did not confine itself to the killing fields.

We heard later that night that young Jack Smith, who was half Arapaho, had surrendered with Charlie Bent when the attack began. He was sitting in a lodge, resting briefly with his father, John, and old Jim Beckwourth, when a group of about 15 soldiers from the Third Colorado Unit appeared. After they entered the lodge, old John Smith heard a voice beckon him outside. As he went outside, a pistol was fired through an opening cut in the lodge—his son, Jack, had been shot in the head.

Charlie Bent was to be their next victim, but soldiers from New Mexico were camped with Chivington, and they knew the Bent family well. They prevented Charlie's execution. With the help of Jim Beckwourth, they hid Charlie for the remainder of that bloody night and released him the following day. What happened next had far-reaching consequences. After witnessing the mass slaughter of his mother's people and his narrow escape from his own execution, Charlie Bent renounced his white heritage and became the scourge of every white person in the eastern plains of Colorado, Kansas, and Nebraska. He lived as a warrior with us until his death in 1868.

The 29th day of November was now over, but the darkness that fell was not the night. It was Death, and it draped late autumn's sky with the color of mourning, and its landscape of soft white and brown hues was forever changed to red.

Only the wind's sound broke nighttime's stillness as it moaned through the sage and prairie grass. We made the only other sounds penetrating that frozen evening as we sought refuge from the army and the weather. Glowing like a million incandescent candles, the stars filling the western sky guided us from Sand Creek's slaughter. Each mile seemed a hundred as, cold and wounded, we trudged our way north to seek help from other bands.

Unsure of his own fate, George Bent pondered his next steps and wondered about his half brother Charlie's whereabouts. Bent walked much of the trip with a rifle ball still imbedded in his hip. Eventually, warriors from Black Kettle's camp found him. These outriders were part of a large hunting party the army had sent away days before their attack on the village. Chivington knew his attack on our village would easily succeed if most of the warriors were absent. From a distance, these warriors watched the desperate fighting but were powerless to help.

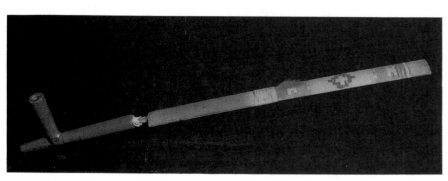

Lakota pipe and stem

Little Bear, myself, and other warriors who were in Black Kettle's camp acted as a rear guard for those who escaped to the prairie's cold, harsh safety. We watched as the wounded were either carried or made their own way across the open plains. There were few blankets and fewer buffalo robes to warm these Cheyenne. They were unaware of what danger lay ahead or whether they were being followed by Chivington's troops. Above all else, they dared not rest or light the fires they so desperately needed—but fires of hate burned in their hearts. For our people, the cold darkness surrounding us seemed eternal. Each step of our journey north ignited another reason to smoke the ceremonial pipe—the occasion would be war.

The majority of Black Kettle's band now thought only of war. Such thoughts followed every step of our way to the South Fork of the Smoky Hill River, until we encountered outriders from the Cheyenne camp we sought, near a place called Bunch of Timbers. They rushed food to us to feed us. We had not eaten in almost three days. As we filled our empty stomachs, wood was thrown on the lodge fires to warm us. As the shock of our ordeal subsided, we vented our anger and frustrations against our own leaders. Many of us blamed Black Kettle for the massacre because he was our chief. Around the council fires many of our people howled him down, and we removed Black Kettle as chief of our band. We elected Leg-in-the-Water in his place. Over time, we realized that Black Kettle's striving for peace and believing the white man were his only sins. Within six weeks, Black Kettle was again our chief. Leg-in-the-Water also stayed with the band. There was no dishonor in anything he did when he was chief. We Tse Tse Stus admitted we had made a mistake in removing Black Kettle.

After a few days of rest and recuperation, we moved northeastward to the Solomon River, in present-day Kansas, where the Sioux were encamped. From there, runners were sent across the Great Plains to other tribes of Sioux, Cheyenne, and Arapaho. Their message: Assemble in council to talk of war against the whites. Before the council met, however, George Bent chose to return to his father's ranch. His wounds were painful, and his trip from the Cheyenne camp was tortuous. With the help of his brother-in-law, Edmond Guerrier, Bent finally found rest and much-needed medical attention in the comfort of his father's home.

Years later, I was told by George that Robert and his half brother, Charlie, had reached the ranch a few days prior to his arrival. After a few days' shelter in the family home and much discussion, George decided to return to his mother's people, the Cheyenne. He took with him Charlie; his sister, Julia; and his stepmother, Yellow Woman. During their brief stay at their father's ranch, George and Charlie informed the elder William Bent, Little White Man, that they had renounced their white heritage after nearly being murdered by his race. Little White Man listened patiently to his sons.

William Bent was frightened and saddened at the unbelievable changes he saw in Charlie. Only a few years before, this youngest Bent had exhibited the curiosity and laughter of a child. What stood before William Bent now was a 15-year-old warrior. His brown eyes now simmered in dark brooding pools of hatred. Anger and a thirst for revenge replaced the laughter of his childhood. His voracious need for revenge became a holy quest. He never again returned to the Bent ranch as a son, although he once returned in an attempt to kill his father. William also saw the anger in George's eyes. Furthermore, he observed in George's eyes confusion, frustration, and hatred for the deeds men do, but he did not see the same venom that was consuming Charlie.

Only Mary and Robert Bent chose to remain in their father's world. In her sorrow and anger, Yellow Woman vowed never again to live in the white world. Julia had already married Edmond Guerrier and chose to live with him and the Cheyenne. The dawn witnessed the last vestige of the Bent family, their final communion grown from Sand Creek's carnage. Little White Man experienced a loneliness he had not felt since the death of his first wife, Owl Woman. Not only had this incident taken his family from him, but the West and the nation had irreparably lost peace with the Indian nations of Sioux, Cheyenne, and Arapaho. Its reverberation would culminate 12 years later near a river named Little Big Horn.

A few days before George and Charlie Bent returned to us and the Sioux camp on the Smoky Hill River, Chivington triumphantly marched his troops into Denver. Throngs of the "Queen City's" citizens welcomed the Third Colorado Volunteers as they displayed their profane trophies of scalps, body parts, and new "tobacco pouches" made from body parts.

News of their "victory" at Sand Creek spread faster than rumors of gold strikes in mining camps throughout Colorado. This event found the *Miner's Register* in Central City advocating the poisoning of all

Indians, as had been done in one incident in Minnesota. There, whites had saturated two or three boxes of bread with strychnine and "left the food on the road for the Indians to find. . . . One hundred men, women and children died from the effects of the poison. . . . That is the kind of warfare we approve of, and should be glad to see it introduced here. It is cheaper pecuniary than to kill them with powder and lead."

Mochi was one of our people who chose to go to war. In the 10 years that followed, she constantly engaged in war and raiding parties throughout Colorado, Nebraska, Wyoming, and Kansas. She also married a great war leader of the Bow String Society named Medicine Water, and she gave birth to three of his children, all girls.[2]

Motherhood did little to slow down Mochi. She continued fighting alongside her husband. During one great battle against the Pawnee, Mochi rode through a group of enemy warriors and rescued her brother, who had had his horse shot out from under him. The Cheyenne called this battle "the time in which the girl saved her brother from the Pawnee." But the winds of fortune and time were running out for both Mochi and Medicine Water.

In mid-September of 1874, Mochi and Medicine Water were roaming the Smokey Hill River area of western Kansas. Late on a hot summer day, her war party attacked a white family named German, who were traveling to Colorado from Georgia. Mochi killed John German, his wife, and his oldest daughter. The four other girls were taken prisoner. Cheyenne war customs forbade them to take any male prisoners. Two other women were killed in the initial attack. Their deaths were merciful compared to the ordeal their four remaining daughters endured. When word of the killings and the girls' abduction reached the army, Colonel Nelson Miles ordered his troops to step up their patrols. Until the German sisters were found and their kidnappers brought to justice, Miles would not let his troops or the Cheyenne rest. It was the beginning of the end for Mochi, Medicine Water, and the Cheyenne's last war in the southern plains.

For two months, Mochi and Medicine Water avoided capture. They and their white captives suffered many hardships. Game was extremely scarce—the white buffalo hunters of that era had all but exterminated the large herds. To Mochi, the appearance of Miles's pursuing troops seemed to replace the buffalo's disappearance throughout the countryside. Mochi and Medicine Water were constantly on the run.

Finally, in April of 1875, Mochi and the last holdouts of the warring Southern Tse Tse Stus surrendered at the Darlington Agency (near present-day El Reno, Oklahoma). Half-starved and aged beyond her 34 years, Mochi's ordeal had not yet ended. The army deemed her so dangerous that they ordered Mochi—and Medicine Water and 29 other Tse Tse Stus—to be chained and ironed. Without trial or tribunal, the army transported them by train to St. Augustine, Florida, where they were imprisoned in a

300-year-old Spanish fort. Mochi and the others thought that they had been brought there to die.

Mochi said that she sat in her jail cell awaiting Death. She knew it was near, for she had just seen the first of the Four Great Rivers one crosses to reach the route of Seyon, the Place of the Dead. She had heard the ve hoes (white men) call this river "ocean," and its overwhelming vastness lay just beyond her barred windows. The salt spray and the roar of the changing tides on the beach beyond the old Spanish fort's outer walls filled her every sense. She must have wondered about the other three rivers she would eventually cross. Mochi smelled Death's malevolent odor in every corner of her dank, mildewed cell. She was preparing herself for Death, as surely as her captors were planning it: Had not her white soldier guards readied her for this journey by cutting off her long, raven hair? Was this not the act of mourning to her people, the Tse Tse Stus? Yet Mochi held no fear of this journey. As a warrior, she had escaped Death's ever-beckoning arms for years on the battlefields of the Great Plains. She had been preparing herself, since growing up in the land whites called Wyoming and Colorado, for the time when Death comes, as it comes to all.

From her small, damp cell, Mochi may have thought about dying in this strange place. The Tse Tse Stus warrior's belief held that death in battle was acceptable, imprisonment was not. Mochi's new surroundings held no comfort for her mind nor body. Only the nearness of her captured husband, Medicine Water, brought her peace.

With chains and the degradation of being punished for speaking her own language, observing her own religion, and dressing in her native dress, Mochi endured her three years of imprisonment. She was the only Native American woman in U.S. history to be sent to prison as a prisoner of war. Although they attempted to change her in all ways, the U.S. Army and the dank, damp cell that held her, succeeded only in breaking her health—but they could not break her spirit.

Mochi and Medicine Water were released in 1878 and sent back to present-day Clinton, Oklahoma. In 1881, Mochi died peacefully, surrounded by her family. She was buried on a high mound, thus securing her journey across the Four Great Rivers and her passageway across the Milky Way, to the Place of the Dead called Seyon. For those Tse Tse Stus who still tell the old tales, the memory of Mochi is alive, for it is said, "As long as your name is spoken, you will never die."

Fort Marion prisoners (taken in 1875). Back row, left to right: Mochi (Buffalo Calf Woman); her husband, Medicine Water. Front row: Black Horse's wife, Wyo (not a prisoner); Black Horse; and Minimic. Photograph courtesy of Castillo de San Marcus National Park

After Old Nam Shim had finished this story, everyone sat quietly for some time. It was a time of quiet reflection for the old man. Shadow, though, wanted to know more about her people's history. She also was curious about the way some of Old Nam Shim's listeners had reacted to his story of Sand Creek.

"Nam Shim," asked Shadow, "why did the older people get up and walk away while you were telling the story?"

"They were not being rude, Little One. In our old ways, if something is unpleasant, or if someone is saying something that is unpleasant to us, it is our custom to just walk away quietly. This story touches the heart of all our people. Many of those who walked away lost relatives at Sand Creek—fathers, mothers, uncles, aunts, grandfathers, and grandmothers. The story is sometimes too hard for them to hear because it is so deeply felt in their hearts.

"Sometimes when the people from the Bureau of Indian Affairs come for a town meeting and want to tell us to do things that we do not want to do, some of us simply say nothing and walk away. That is our old way. Today the younger people speak up. This is okay, too, but it is not our old way. Do you understand, Shadow?"

"Yes, Nam Shim, but could you please tell me about something that has always bothered me? How did we come to be in this place we call the Reservation? And how come there's all this talk about the Northern Cheyenne and the Southern Cheyenne? Are there other Cheyenne?"

"We were put on this Reservation by the government in 1878. We were told we had to live here, but many of us were sent to what is now Oklahoma. So, yes, Shadow, there are many of our relatives down in Oklahoma. Their story is our story, and it happened after Sand Creek."

Notes

[1]Mo ke and Mó'kĕ huduovse are Cheyenne spellings for the woman whose name translates to English as Buffalo Calf Woman. We are using the spelling *Mochi* in this book because that is the way it is spelled in several historical documents, including Fort Marion records.

[2]The first child born was named Red Woman. She died as a young woman. No one knows the cause of her death. The other two daughters were Standing Bird and Sprinkle Horse Woman, and they lived to be very old.

Discussion and Activities

Goals

■ Understand the massacre at Sand Creek from the Cheyenne point of view.

■ Identify the key events and participants in the massacre.

Discussion Questions

1. Describe a Cheyenne birth and the customs that were followed to protect the baby after the birth.

    Answer: The midwives immediately grease and powder the baby's body with finely ground, dried manure, and decayed cottonwood pulp to protect the baby from evil. Once the placenta is expelled, the midwives place it in a deerskin bag; the Tse Tse Stus believe that if they bury the placenta, the baby will die, so the bag was tied to a tree. Once the umbilical cord has been separated from the baby, the midwives cut it in half and wrap one-half in a soft piece of beaded buckskin, which is then shaped into a pouch and sewn together. The grandmother beads the other half of the umbilical cord and places it inside the cradle to ensure long life and protection from evil spirits. She places a piece of beaded umbilical cord of an animal on the outside of the cradle to fool any evil spirits that might come visiting. A design is beaded onto a deerskin pouch, which contains the baby's umbilical cord.

2. What are the lessons taught to young Cheyenne children?

    Answer: Cheyenne history and customs, through the oral tradition of storytelling.

3. How many bands of Cheyenne were camped out at Sand Creek for the winter?

    Answer: 5.

4. How many lodges of Arapaho were camped there?

    Answer: 10.

5. Why did the village feel that their safety was ensured?

    Answer: They were flying the flag of the United States over the village.

6. Were there any soldiers in the Cheyenne village?

    Answer: Yes, Private David Louderback. He was there along with interpreter John Smith; his son, Jack Smith; Charlie Bent; and a teamster named Clark, who was trading with the Cheyenne and Arapaho.

7. What was the first unusual sound the village heard?

    Answer: Thundering hooves. At first the Cheyenne thought the noise to be a large herd of buffalo.

8. Describe the attack.

    Answer: See pages pp. 66–72.

---

9. How many Cheyenne and Arapaho were killed at Sand Creek?

> *Answer:* 137.

10. Name the Cheyenne woman who became a warrior at Sand Creek.

> *Answer:* Mochi, also called Buffalo Calf Woman.

11. What officer from Chivington's troops ordered his men not to fire at the Indians and at one point positioned his troops between the fleeing Cheyenne and Chivington's troops?

> *Answer:* Captain Silas Soule.

12. What happened to Jack Smith after he was taken prisoner by Chivington's troops?

> *Answer:* He was executed.

13. What happened to Black Kettle's wife?

> *Answer:* She survived the massacre even though she was shot nine times.

14. What time of year, in the Cheyenne calendar, did the massacre take place?

> *Answer:* The Time of the Hard-Face Moon (November).

15. How did Mochi manage to escape? How was she finally captured?

> *Answer:* She fought her way up the dry riverbed and escaped. She surrendered after 10 years of fighting.

16. What made Mochi think she was going to die when she was taken to the prison in Florida?

> *Answer:* The guards had cut her hair, which is a sign of mourning for Cheyenne; and when she saw the Atlantic Ocean, she thought she was seeing the first of the Four Great Rivers to cross to Seyon, the Place of the Dead.

Things to Do

Discussion Activity

In describing the massacre, Nam Shim had used the phrase "Violence begot more violence." Brainstorm with students about the meaning of this phrase. Relate it to experiences that they can personally identify with, such as one student punching another student and the situation quickly escalating into a fight.

Writing Activity

In the wars that took place over the several decades after Sand Creek, revenge played a large part in the escalation of violence. Have students write in their own words what revenge means and the role it played in the events narrated in this chapter. Have students keep their writing to use in the activities in chapter seven.

Library Research

Have students research individually or in small groups information on the following:

■ The Bent family played a large role in the events of Cheyenne history and Colorado history. Have students research the family members: William, Charles, George, Robert, and Mary.

■ The BIA (Bureau of Indian Affairs) was established during this time. Have students research this agency (its origins, who governed it, etc.). From this information, have students comment on why the Indians were so negative towards this agency.

■ To give students a perspective of what Colorado, and the other plains states (territories), were like at this time, have students research what was then happening in the cities and territories, particularly Denver, Kansas, and Oklahoma.

Class Bulletin Board

Locate the following on the map: Sand Creek; Wyoming, which the Tse Tse Stus called Yellowstone; Smoky Hill River; Solomon River; Kansas; Denver; El Reno, Oklahoma; St. Augustine, Florida; Clinton, Oklahoma.

Add the results of the students' library research to the class bulletin board.

7

The War

Now many whites, including some in the military, thought that what Chivington had done was extremely evil.

The Commission for the Conduct of War concluded its hearings on the 76th day of its existence. From February 9 through May 30, 1865, the commission heard hundreds of hours of testimony and read affidavits from dozens of witnesses. Ulysses S. Grant, Commanding General of the Union Army, said that Chivington's actions amounted to nothing more than murder. Joseph Holt, the U.S. Army's Judge Advocate General, stated that it was a "cowardly and cold-blooded slaughter, sufficient to cover its perpetrators with indelible infamy and the face of every American with shame and indignation."

When the hearings were over, it was obvious to the commission and others that there had indeed been a tragic and brutal massacre of our people and of the Arapaho at a place called Sand Creek. It was also obvious that no charges would ever be filed against any of the men responsible for this crime against humanity, especially Shoup and Chivington. They were regarded too highly by men in high places.

Not even Silas Soule's killer was brought to justice. Soule was the friend of Tall Chief Wynkoop who refused to fire on our people at Sand Creek. A soldier named Squiers lured Soule away from his home in Denver while he was the Provost Marshall. He did this by firing his pistol into the air to make it sound like there was trouble outside. As Provost Marshall, it was Soule's duty to investigate any disturbance like this with the local sheriff or marshall. This was a time of war, not only the war that began with our people, but of the white man's Civil War. As Soule went out into the Denver streets, Squiers ambushed Soule and shot him through the head. Before he died, though, Soule wounded Squiers. Tall Chief Wynkoop told me this story.

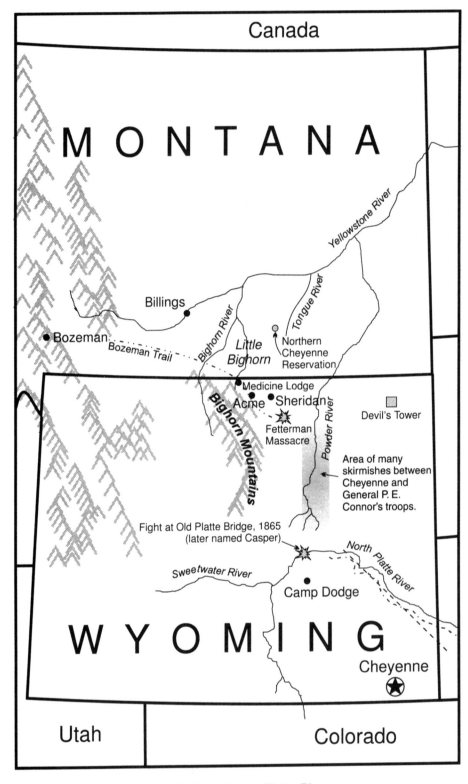

Canada

MONTANA

Yellowstone River

Billings

Bozeman

Bozeman Trail

Bighorn River

Little Bighorn

Tongue River

Northern Cheyenne Reservation

Medicine Lodge

Acme

Sheridan

Bighorn Mountains

Fetterman Massacre

Powder River

Devil's Tower

Area of many skirmishes between Cheyenne and General P. E. Connor's troops.

Fight at Old Platte Bridge, 1865 (later named Casper)

North Platte River

Sweetwater River

Camp Dodge

WYOMING

Cheyenne

Utah

Colorado

- - - - - - -   Cheyenne route followed North Platte River
· - · - · - · -   North Platte Road

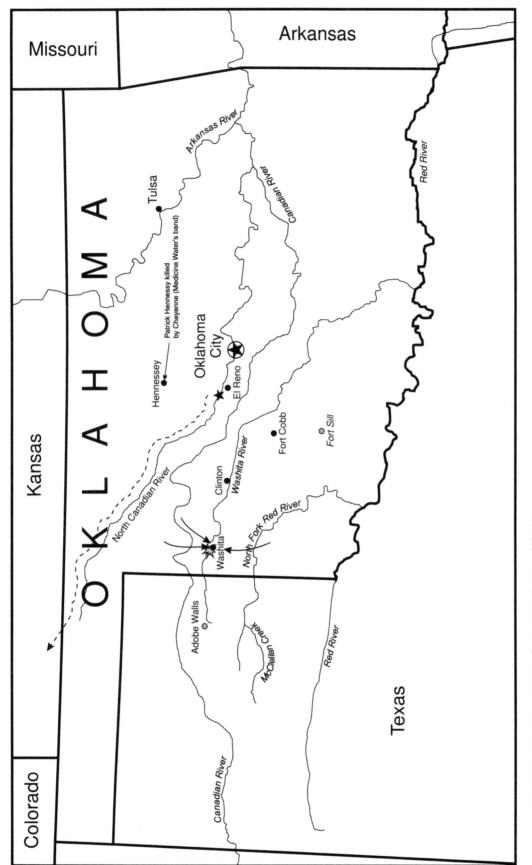

Missouri

Arkansas

Kansas

O K L A H O M A

Colorado

Texas

Tulsa

Arkansas River

Canadian River

Red River

Patrick Hennessy killed
by Cheyenne (Medicine Water's band)

Oklahoma
City

Hennessey

El Reno

Fort Cobb

Fort Sill

Clinton

Washita River

North Canadian River

North Fork Red River

Washita

Adobe Walls

McClellan Creek

Red River

Canadian River

→ Indicates 3-prong attack by Custer on village at Washita.

--→ Black Horse escape route, 1875

★ Indicates where Mochi was sentenced to prison and Black Horse made his escape.

◉ Indicates a fort.

The War

He also told me that almost immediately after Soule's murder, Squiers deserted the Colorado Second Infantry and fled to Las Vegas, New Mexico. While a search for him spread throughout Colorado, someone in New Mexico recognized him and sent a letter to Denver telling of his whereabouts. The army ordered First Lieutenant James D. Cannon to arrest him for Soule's murder and for desertion.

Cannon and a small detachment of men took the long, arduous trail down to northern New Mexico. After leaving Trinidad, Colorado, they rode to the summit of Raton Pass. Lined on either side by spruce- and pine-covered mountains, this pass descends into New Mexico, where the prairie desert comes into full view for hundreds of square miles.

When Cannon and his men arrived in Las Vegas, they promptly arrested Squiers without incident. The soldier offered no resistance, but hinted that the lieutenant didn't know what he was getting into. Squiers's threats didn't bother the lieutenant. Cannon had also been at Sand Creek, and he, too, found the courage to testify against Chivington. He was a man of great courage. It was Cannon's men, the New Mexico Volunteers, who helped save Charlie Bent from execution on the night of November 29, 1864, in the midst of men who outnumbered his troops, and he stood up for what he believed. To Cannon, men like Squiers were scum, and he strongly felt that the army should get rid of them by use of rope or bullet.

When Cannon returned Squiers to Denver in midsummer, murder happened again. On July 14, 1865, authorities found 24-year-old James D. Cannon dead in his Denver hotel room. And Squiers, who had been incarcerated in Denver's city jail, had disappeared! The suspected cause of Cannon's death was poison. He was the second officer murdered after testifying against Chivington and the others. The authorities never arrested anyone in connection with his death, and Squiers fled to California, where he successfully eluded being brought to justice.

During these chaotic and violent months in 1865, the Cheyenne were still raiding eastern Colorado and the Nebraska and Kansas western plains. The events that started on an almost dry riverbed called Sand Creek were now spilling over into Wyoming and the Dakotas.

Shortly after Julesburg had been sacked a second time, I went north to the Powder River areas of South Dakota and Wyoming with the Cheyenne who had joined up with the Sioux. There, major skirmishes between the U.S. Army and the Sioux and Cheyenne became more frequent. In February 1865, the Southern Cheyenne and Red Cloud's Oglala Sioux gathered in northwestern Nebraska and planned new raids against the army. It was in this massive camp that we first looked upon our Northern Cheyenne brothers. The differences in appearance and language between our two tribes of the ancient Tse Tse Stus amazed all of us who had lived in the south.

Our northern brothers were dressed differently from us and looked strange to our eyes. We wore cloth blankets, cloth leggings, and other things made by whites, but the Northern Tse Tse Stus were dressed in buffalo robes and buckskin leggings. Their braided hair was wrapped in strips of buckskin that were painted red. Unlike us, they wore crow feathers instead of eagle feathers on their heads, with the ends of those feathers cut off in a peculiar manner. They looked much wilder than any of us and kept up all the old customs because they had not come into contact with the whites. They were more like the Sioux in habits and appearance. It had been almost 40 years since our two tribes separated.[1] I was far too young at the time to remember that our Southern Tse Tse Stus once looked like our Northern brothers.

During winter, the tribes moved their camps often to avoid detection. They moved again when spring made its way into this northern land, this time to the basin of Wyoming's Big Horn Mountains. From there, war parties began raiding the North Platte Road. The Cheyenne, Arapaho, and Sioux attacked numerous stage stops and small army garrisons throughout the spring, including Camp Dodge, located about 30 miles south of present day Casper, Wyoming.

On July 25, more than 1,000 Sioux and Cheyenne attacked two troops of cavalry at Old Platte Bridge, a small settlement. The battle filled the hot, clear day with so much gunsmoke and dust that visibility was cut down to about a dozen yards. Few soldiers survived. One who did not was Lieutenant Caspar Collins. During the thick of battle, he was shot in the forehead with an arrow. Shortly thereafter, the Wyoming Territory renamed Old Platte Bridge, in his honor, but misspelled his name—Casper.

By now, thousands of U.S. troops were arriving from the Civil War's eastern battlefields to put down this new western Indian war. Up to this time, all efforts to quell the uprising had failed, and western and eastern newspapers alike had called for a change of tactics and command. The citizens demanded an experienced Indian fighter. More important, big businesses demanded help in clearing the West of Indians. Months earlier, the Overland Stage Company exerted its influential pressure on the U.S. War Department for an experienced Indian fighter. They sent Brigadier General P. E. Connor from his Utah command to chase us.

Patrick Edward Connor was not a large man. He had gained a big reputation for being an Indian fighter by what he did in Utah. In the Time of the Hoop Moon (Hohtséeše'he, January) of 1863, on the banks of Utah's Bear River, he and his men surprised a large village of Paiutes and Shoshone Indians. They slaughtered 278 people, including many women and children. Through this carnage, Connor emerged a hero of the western frontier. Much to Chivington's dismay, who disliked Connor because of his good reputation as an Indian fighter, the general soon became popular in Colorado and Nebraska.

Between April and May of 1865, General Connor ordered details of troops to protect the stage lines still operating in these areas. According to initial observations, the deployment of his troops seemed to have discouraged Indians raids. The army hadn't realized that the Indians were still in winter camp. By mid-May, our tribes renewed their attacks on the roads with a boldness never before witnessed. The guerrilla-style warfare of the Cheyenne, Arapaho, and Sioux prevented Connor from stopping their raids. After the Indians soundly defeated Lieutenant Caspar Collins's two troops of cavalry at Old Platte Bridge, Wyoming, white settlers began to panic. Had we, the Cheyenne and the Sioux, continued our raids until August, the roads probably would have been closed for years. Fortunately for the whites, we camped along the Powder River and held our ritual summer medicine ceremonies. Connor had time to regroup. With his large force, he built a stockade near a favorite river crossing of the Sioux and Cheyenne. With his forces. as well as a small army of Pawnee and Omaha Indian scouts, Connor implemented a change of tactics. While the general built his fort, the Pawnees watched for Cheyenne and Sioux.

These Indians set to their task well. In late summer in Wyoming, the Pawnee lured about 30 Cheyenne into one of their ambushes. George Bent's stepmother, Yellow Woman, was among them. The Pawnee dressed themselves as Sioux and signaled the Cheyenne with their blankets: "We are friends; come nearer." As the Cheyenne rode closer, they fell into the Pawnee's ambush. Five Cheyenne were killed. That night, the Pawnee scouts held a scalp dance at General Connor's camp. Among the freshly severed scalp locks they paraded on a stick as they sang was that of Yellow Woman.

The war in the Wyoming plains was now escalating. A few days after Yellow Woman's death, I heard that Connor and his troops had surprised a large Arapaho camp on Wolf Creek. His Pawnee and Omaha Indian scouts raided their pony herd, and a furious battle ensued. Although taken off guard, the infuriated Arapaho were able to turn back Connor's forces. The price they paid was high. The Arapaho lost most of their pony herd and 60 of their scalps to their Pawnee enemies. It was Connor's only successful engagement in Wyoming, largely caused by the fighting skills of his Pawnee and Omaha scouts.

In Colorado, Black Kettle's Southern Cheyenne still sought peace. In October 1865, through the efforts of their friend and brother William Bent, the Cheyenne signed a treaty with the whites they no longer trusted. Throughout the Dakota Territory, skirmishes between the Cheyenne, Sioux, and the army continued well into the next year in places called Medicine Lodge and Powder River. The army avoided major disasters only because of our inadequate firepower.

Notes

[1]Letter from George Bent to George Hyde, from George Hyde, *The Life of George Bent, Written from His Letters*. (Norman, Oklahoma: University of Oklahoma Press.)

Discussion and Activities

Goals

- Understand how the massacre at Sand Creek touched off the beginning of a 12-year war.

- Recount the actions the Cheyenne warriors took in seeking revenge.

Discussion Questions

1. Not all officers were pleased with Chivington's actions at Sand Creek. What two officers spoke out against him?

    Answer: Captain Silas Soule and First Lieutenant James D. Cannon.

2. What eventually happened to these two outspoken men?

    Answer: Both men were murdered.

3. When the hearings were over and all affidavits were taken, the commission investigating the massacre at Sand Creek acknowledged that a tremendous wrong had been done. Yet, no charges were ever brought against any of the officers. Why?

    Answer: Those responsible were regarded too highly by men in high places.

4. In February of 1865, the Southern Cheyenne met their Northern Cheyenne brothers for the first time in 40 years. The differences were quite striking. What were those differences?

    Answer: Clothing—Southern Cheyenne wore cloth blankets, cloth leggings, and other things made by whites, but the Northern Cheyenne dressed in buffalo robes and buckskin leggings. They also braided their hair and wrapped it in strips of buckskin that were painted red. They wore crow feathers instead of the eagle feathers common among the Southern Cheyenne. Their language was also different.

5. What were some of the major skirmishes that took place during these wars?

    Answer: Julesburg, Old Platte Bridge, Camp Dodge, Powder River, and Medicine Lodge.

Things to Do

Class Discussion

This chapter mentions some of the cultural differences within the Cheyenne people. Differences between the Northern Cheyenne and the Southern Cheyenne were caused by years of separation. Explain to students that these wars involved many Native American cultural groups, some of whom united in their efforts against the white man.

Geography Activity

Calculate the area covered by these wars in square miles. Look at a topographical map and describe what the terrain of the land was like. Discuss the problems both sides would have experienced when fighting battles in this area.

Library Research

For this type of war, the weapons were very different from the ones used in modern wars. Have students research weapons and warfare used during the Indian wars. Based on their research, have students draw the weapons used in these battles. Add their drawings to the class bulletin board.

Class Bulletin Board

Locate the following on the map: Trinidad and Julesburg, Colorado; Las Vegas, New Mexico; Casper, Wyoming; Raton Pass; Nebraska; the Dakotas; Utah; Wolf Creek; Powder River; Big Horn Mountains. Recount the events of this chapter, this time using the map to plot the locations of the battles.

Detail of woman's engraved silver belt

8

The Beginning of the End

The U.S. government continued its buildup of supplies and troops in Wyoming's frontier. Their orders: Build a string of forts along the Bozeman Trail. "The Trail," founded by cattleman John Bozeman, was the most direct route to Montana's gold fields. This new intrusion of white miners into the Sioux and Northern Cheyenne's heartland resulted in America's first massacre of soldiers from which no survivors emerged.

In 1866, the U.S. Army established Fort Phil Kearny near present-day Sheridan, Wyoming. Commanded by Colonel Henry B. Carrington, its specific purpose was to protect Bozeman Trail travelers from hostile attack. During the fort's short existence, work parties from the post were continually attacked and harassed by the Lakota (Sioux) and Cheyenne. In one such engagement, Governor Evan's old informant, Bob North, led a charge against the army with an Arapaho war party. Protecting themselves, Fort Phil Kearny's workmen fired on North, shooting a finger from his left hand. He survived northern Wyoming's war but was hanged in Kansas three years later, along with his wife, by vigilantes.

Late autumn of 1866 had frozen the ground around Fort Phil Kearny. With the arrival of winter's first day, snow covered the mountains. Though the morning was quite pleasant, we could tell from the smell in the air that bad weather would soon be upon us. Our scouts watched the white soldiers work, cutting wood, in their shirts the army called "blouses." The snow from around the fort had melted, but deep drifts of winter's white harvest still lay in the woods as Big Piney Creek remained motionless in its frozen state. Just before the sun was straight up in the sky, we Cheyenne, along with the Sioux, attacked the wood-cutting party. Colonel Carrington ordered Captain William Fetterman to "support the wood train . . . relieve it and report to me. Do not engage or pursue Indians at its expense. Under no circumstances pursue over the ridge, that is, Lodge Trail Ridge."

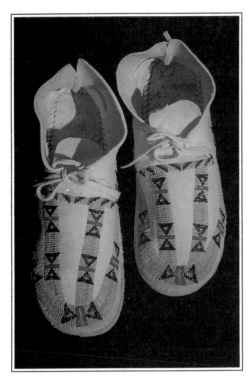

Now this Captain William Fetterman, a highly decorated Civil War veteran before his transfer to Fort Phil Kearny, distinguished himself in battles called Stone's River, Kennesaw Mountain, and Peach Tree Creek, but he had never before fought Indians. Upon his arrival at Fort Phil Kearny, Fetterman renewed an old friendship with Captain Frederick Brown. The two men knew each other from their Ohio days and the Civil War. Brown immediately oriented Fetterman to life at the fort and disclosed his personal dislike for its commanding officer. It didn't take long for his friend to agree. His disdain for the Sioux and Cheyenne was obvious too. He once bragged that he could take 80 men and march through the entire Sioux nation.

The price of Fetterman's arrogance was his life. When he left Fort Phil Kearny's gates, he and the 80 men of his command went to relieve the wood-cutting party. We lured the vainglorious captain, who disregarded his specific orders from Colonel Carrington, into an ambush. Fetterman and his troops followed Sioux decoys beyond Lodge Trail Ridge. When they reached the ridge's top, they met a force of more than 1,000 Sioux, Cheyenne, and Arapaho warriors. The battle lasted less than an hour. When it was over, Fetterman and his command of 80 men were dead! No wounded or prisoners survived winter's first day of 1866. Until Custer's death nine and one-half years later, this was the U. S. Army's worst defeat by Indians. Sand Creek had taught us well: All in Fetterman's command were mutilated.

The war with the Northern Cheyenne and Sioux continued for two more years. However, two months prior to Fetterman's death, George Bent returned to Black Kettle's Southern Cheyenne village and married the old chief's niece, Magpie. During this period, Tall Chief Wynkoop resigned his army commission and became the Southern Cheyenne and Arapaho's Indian Agent. Through Wynkoop's work and respect for a people he loved, an uneasy peace came to this land. The tranquility of that fragile treaty at Medicine Lodge was lost for a while when an eastern general, Winfield Scott Hancock, burned a Cheyenne village.

Then, on November 6, 1868, something extraordinary happened. In Wyoming's Powder River area, the U. S. Army, for the first time in its history, was forced to make peace with the Sioux nation. In the two years since Fetterman's disaster, Chief Red Cloud, his Oglalas tribe, and we Cheyenne outmaneuvered and outfought the U. S. Army. President Andrew Johnson and the Congress demanded that Ulysses S. Grant's best friend, William Tecumseh Sherman, the man who had led one of the most powerful armies in history on a path of destruction from Atlanta to the sea only four years earlier, make peace with an enemy his troops could not defeat.

Feeling that a lasting peace was at hand, exactly four years to the day after the massacre at Sand Creek, Edward Wynkoop resigned his position as Indian Agent. He was unaware that history had already repeated itself two days prior to his resignation. On November 27, 1868, Black Kettle and his people were again at peace with the United States and were camped by a river they called Washita, in what is now western Oklahoma. This time, George Bent and Magpie, his wife, were not present in the village. Whether memories of what happened at Sand Creek almost four years before made him leave, or whether Maheo had intervened and this was not his day to die is unknown, but George and his wife were safely on their way to visit his father in Colorado. There were other survivors of Sand Creek's tragedy, though, who were not as fortunate. Out of his most horrible nightmares, Black Kettle and his wife awoke to the reality—it was happening again! Between the first light and the dawn, another U.S. cavalry troop, led by Lieutenant Colonel George Armstrong Custer, charged into their village and killed 101 people, most of whom were again women and children running for cover.

As before at Sand Creek, an American flag flew over their village for protection that never came. This time, Black Kettle and his wife did not survive. When the shooting started, Black Kettle jumped on his horse and pulled his wife up behind him in a desperate attempt to escape. It was too late, though. He and his wife, Medicine Calf, were shot to pieces. Their lifeless bodies fell into the Washita's cold, shallow waters. While the fight for survival continued among the living, Death's indignities were splashed on Black Kettle and Medicine Calf by the hooves of horses caught in combat. Soon after, one of Custer's soldiers appeared with a knife in his hand and cut off the great chief's scalp. The Cheyenne had lost a great chief, and Wynkoop had lost a very dear friend.

Again, Little One, not all who were with Custer were evil. Along with Custer and his Seventh Cavalry was a detachment of the Ninth Cavalry, the Buffalo Soldiers. These were African American troops who were sent to the West during the Civil War. While Custer's men were killing every Cheyenne in sight, one of the Buffalo Soldiers came upon two small Cheyenne girls and their mother. His gun was drawn from its holster, but instead of shooting the three, he holstered his gun, dismounted his horse, and hid the three from harm. Shadow, many years later, one of the little girls, who was by then a woman, came into the Darlington Agency in El Reno, Oklahoma, for her commodities. She saw this same man sitting on the store's porch. She stared at him for a long time. Finally, she approached him and asked him if he had been with Custer at the Washita River. He said yes. The woman, who was the little girl, told him who she was and then asked him, "Why did you hide us and not shoot us?" He simply said, "I had a wife and children your ages. I don't make war on women and children."

His story is still told among our people.

Custer and his men did not stop their slaughter with human beings. He and his men shot between 600 and 900 ponies, and then burned all the Cheyenne lodges and their possessions. Custer then retreated, leaving 20 of his own soldiers behind. They were trapped in the remains of the village. The enraged Cheyenne cut them to pieces. Six years later, on June 25, 1876, Custer and 225 men of the U.S. Seventh Cavalry paid for the sins he committed on the banks of the Washita River. They all died at the hands of the Cheyenne and Sioux near a river in Montana called Little Big Horn. It was a great day for the Indians, but a bad one for Custer's family. Accompanying George Custer on that fateful day were his two brothers, Tom and Boston. It was the worst defeat in the U.S. Army's history at the hands of Native American people. It was the second battle in which there were no white survivors!

Little One, the atrocities committed against the Cheyenne and Arapaho neither began nor ended with Sand Creek, nor did the depredations committed against the innocent whites who inadvertently found themselves in the middle of a war. History's unwritten rule reflects that the vanquished shall inherit only misery and despair, and their conquerors shall rejoice in the women's lamentation, for their mourning shall be a sweet song of tribute.

In the years between Custer's attack at the Washita River and his death at Little Big Horn, the government sent most of the Southern Cheyenne to various reservations established under the guidance of the Friends of Society. President Ulysses S. Grant's administration created the Indian Territory in what is presently the state of Oklahoma. Their concept of a reservation and its reality were a huge shock to us Cheyenne. The Indian Territory's hot and exceptionally arid climate proved alien compared to our traditional prairie land. In some areas, we found the water too brackish for our ponies' survival. Our Quaker agents wanted to transform us into farmers and teach us to perform all sorts of manual labor. These white Christians obviously possessed no knowledge of our customs. They also gave our people instructions in English, but few Cheyenne understood or spoke English. The farming went against hundreds of years of Tse Tse Stus tradition. The Quakers also insisted that our children be sent to agency schools. After months of no cooperation, the Friends finally realized that verbal communication with the Cheyenne might help their problem, so they hired interpreters. Still, even with oral communication available, our warrior societies refused to become farmers. At first there were no open hostilities toward the agency, though their schools remained empty of our children. We remained at peace but were adamant about our children not becoming like any of the whites we had seen and fought for so many years.

In 1870, George Bent and Magpie were among the residents at the first of these agencies, the Darlington Agency. Agent Brinton Darlington, a Quaker for whom the agency was named, hired Bent as an interpreter. There, Bent worked to ensure that no communication gap existed for the Cheyenne and Arapaho in their talks with the whites. Life for George and Magpie remained peaceful and prosperous for about two years. Then, Kiowa warriors arrived at the agency and tried to convince the Cheyenne and Arapaho to go on the warpath with them. The white man's progress created new encroachments on what little remained of their way of life. The Kiowa felt that it was time to rise up and put a halt to those who sought more of their ever-dwindling domain. Tempted as many of the young warriors were, we Tse Tse Stus declined.

Not long after the Kiowa's visit, tensions mounted. Numerous bands of horse thieves, who operated out of Dodge City, Kansas, preyed upon the reservation's pony herds. Completely ruthless, their outlaw raids became more commonplace and violent. Not wanting another war, we Cheyenne complained and asked for protection. Since the beginning of time, though, when man first created war, the story has always been the same—the words of the vanquished have always fallen on deaf ears.

Eventually, the Southern Cheyenne and Arapaho sent a delegation to Washington, D.C., to meet with President Grant. The Great White Father with the Whiskey Breath listened intently to Little Robe and other delegates. He said that he understood their plight and would help them, for he, the Great White Father, knew and despised war more than all others. He reminded them that he had once commanded the largest army the world had ever seen. Grant promised Little Robe and the others protection, but his promise was like the wind in buffalo grass—nothing would come of it.

The following year, as the Iron Horse (ma'aetaemèò'o, the trains of the white man) rode through our traditional lands, the remainder of the last great buffalo herds were literally cut in half by this manmade beast's rails. With the railroad came more white settlers, and even more obscene to us were the organized bands of buffalo hunters. These hunters immediately subjected the southern herd to a slaughter the world has never forgotten. They had come for the hides the great beasts possessed. After they had killed their game and removed the hides, they left the carcasses to rot in the sun. The sight of this senseless slaughter sickened our people, as it beckoned vultures to finish off the hide hunters' claim.

We Cheyenne and our cousins the Arapaho looked on in disbelief. To us, the buffalo represented life itself. It was our belief that the Creator had created the buffalo for our use. We made our lodges, as well as winter moccasins and robes, from the hides for protection against the cold; we also molded shields as well as parfleche cases, saddle covers, and cradles for the young. From the horns of this beast, we sculptured spoons and dishes, and from the head's long hair, we Cheyenne made ropes and lariats. The meat provided the mainstay of our diet, and from the heavy shoulder blades, we Cheyenne carved tools for dressing the hides. The brains, liver, and fat were used in tanning the hides, and the sinew became our thread. We wasted no part of this revered animal. We even used the tail to create handles for clubs and medicine wands, and the hooves produced our glue.

We Cheyenne remained at peace for a time as we witnessed the destruction of our food, clothing, and tools. We hoped President Grant would keep his promise of protection. The raids on our pony herds continued, though, and the buffalo's endless slaughter by white hunters, coupled with our dissatisfaction with the Indian agency's distribution of supplies, finally forced us into action.

When he finished this story, Nam Shim remained quiet awhile and then said, "Little One, I'm very tired now. Tomorrow I will tell you the story of our last fights against the ve hoes (the whites)." Slowly the old man got up, and Shadow rushed over to his side to steady him. She helped Nam Shim into his house, where his grandson's wife slowly helped him to his room. Soon all was quiet, except for the few manmade noises that came from Nam Shim's house.

The following morning all Shadow could think about was the story he would tell her that night. Shadow's thirst for her people's history was now insatiable. She knew that Old Nam Shim would sleep late, so she shared her morning with the "water spirits" of the Tongue River.

Discussion and Activities

Goals

■ Examine the importance of the massacre at Sand Creek to the Cheyenne wars that continued for the next 12 years.

■ Trace the lives of the Cheyenne who survived the massacre at Sand Creek and their trails from Colorado through Kansas, Nebraska, Wyoming, Oklahoma, and Montana.

Discussion Questions

1. What new threat came to the Lakotas and Cheyenne in 1866?

    Answer: A string of forts the army was building along the Bozeman Trail.

2. Why did the Lakotas and Cheyenne see this as a threat?

    Answer: Each time the white man moved farther into their territory and built forts and towns, he was taking their homeland away from them.

3. Captain William Fetterman was transferred to Fort Phil Kearny during the Sioux and Cheyenne wars. What was his opinion on handling the tribes?

    Answer: He said that he could take 80 men and march through the heart of the Sioux (Lakota) territory.

4. What happened to Captain William Fetterman?

    Answer: He and his entire command were massacred in late 1866. It was the first time in the U.S. Army's history that there were no survivors after a battle with Native Americans.

5. What happened on November 6, 1868?

    Answer: The U.S. government was forced to sign a peace treaty with the Sioux (under Chief Red Cloud) because they could not win the war they were presently fighting.

6. What happened to Black Kettle on November 27, 1868, almost four years to the day after the massacre at Sand Creek?

    Answer: He and his people, who again were at peace with the United States, were attacked between first light and dawn by the U.S. Seventh Cavalry under the command of Lieutenant Colonel George Armstrong Custer. One hundred one Cheyenne died that day, including Black Kettle and his wife.

7. Where were the Southern Cheyenne sent after they surrendered?

    Answer: To a reservation in what is now Oklahoma, then called the Indian Territory.

8. Who ran the reservations?

    Answer: The Quakers.

9. What did the Quakers want to transform the Cheyenne into?

    Answer: Farmers.

Things to Do

Discussion/Writing Activity

Ask students to imagine being told that they and their families are going to have to leave their home and move to another country. Everything will be different: the land, the weather, the language, and so on. They will not know anyone, and, at first, will not know the language. Their parents will have to give up their jobs and do something unfamiliar to them. Have students think about this situation for a few minutes and then write what their feelings might be if this really happened. Once they have had time to write, have them share their feelings with the rest of the class. Lead the class in a discussion of what the Native American people must have felt as they were required to do this very same thing when they were moved to reservations.

Library Research

The Native Americans were eventually relocated to reservations. These reservations were often in areas far from the tribe's homeland and therefore, very different from what they had been accustomed to. President Grant's administration created the Indian Territory in what is today Oklahoma. Have students research the geography of Oklahoma and of the plains area of Colorado. What are some of the differences that the Cheyenne people had to deal with? How would this affect their traditional culture?

Pipe bag

Class Bulletin Board

Locate the following on the map: Wyoming; Kansas; Nebraska; Oklahoma; Montana; and the city of Bozeman, Montana.

9

The End of an Era

Old Nam Shim spent the better part of the next day in bed. His tired old body needed rest. His grandson tried to talk him out of telling stories that evening, but his only reply was, "I must, for who will remember the stories if I don't tell them to someone? Young Shadow will listen and learn and tell others when I am gone."

There would be no dissuading him. That night, to the amazement of almost all his listeners, Old Nam Shim picked up the story exactly where he had left off the night before.

In 1874, in the Texas panhandle on Canadian River's South Fork, the hide hunters became even more bold when they established themselves in the heart of Indian hunting grounds. The site they chose was an abandoned trading fort called Adobe Walls, which ironically was built and operated by William Bent as a sometime trading post around 1842. The fort had been deserted for years because Bent thought that it was located too far south for his purposes.

"The hide hunters' presence at this location infuriated a Comanche medicine man named Isatai (whose name translates into English as Rear-End-of-a-Wolf). Isatai claimed that he possessed supernatural powers and could make the white man's bullets useless. Through his oratories and haranguing, this medicine man ignited a warring faction of the Comanches into action. The word soon spread to other tribes—the Kiowa, Arapaho, and Cheyenne. Small bands from each of these tribes finally agreed to make war on these white men who, by 1872–73, had already killed in excess of 200,000 buffalo.

Isatai and a Comanche leader named Quanah planned to raid these hunters. The course of their action called for Comanche, Kiowa, Cheyenne, and Arapaho warriors to attack the buffalo hunters at Adobe

Walls before dawn's first light. Had it not been for the hot Texas night, combined with the thickly insulated adobe walls, causing some of the hunters to sleep just outside in wagons, their scheme might have succeeded. When the combined Indian forces attacked, hunters in the wagons were awakened and began firing back before the Indians could gain entry into the compound.

Inside Bent's old trading post walls, 26 buffalo hunters, including Billy Dixon and future western lawman, gambler, and sports writer Bat Masterson, found themselves greatly outnumbered. Fortunately for the hunters, they possessed an advantage. Within their reach was an amazing arsenal of weapons and ammunition that they used for their methodical slaughter of buffalo. In their well-made plans, the hunters chose the heavily fortified walls for protection against the chance of such an attack. The walls could not be shot through or burned. To make matters worse for our people, the hunters barricaded the closed gates with a heavy pile of buffalo robes and their wagons. The furious fighting lasted for hours. When it was over, not a single white hunter had been killed or wounded, but eleven Indians, including five Cheyenne warriors—Horse Rode, Walks on Ground, Spotted Feathers, Coyote, and Stone Teeth—lay dead within feet of the gates of Adobe Walls. Isatai's medicine had failed. As the Cheyenne and others retreated, they must have thought the meaning of his name appropriate. Before they departed, however, they captured or killed most of the hunters' horses. A few days after the fighting was over, Prairie Chief and a party of Cheyenne returned to Adobe Walls. The hunters had vacated the fort's protection, but they had left behind a gruesome reminder of the fight. Nine heads of the warriors killed had been severed and stuck on boards nailed to a long pole in the ground.

The failure at Adobe Walls quickly disillusioned a majority of the Arapaho warriors who followed Isatai and then returned to the agency. The Cheyenne, though, were eager to continue the fight. They preferred death in battle to death by starvation. On July 3, 1874, near present-day Hennessey, Oklahoma, a Cheyenne war party attacked a freighter named Patrick Hennessy and his small wagon train. Hennessy's friend George Bent warned him not to make the trip. He tried to tell Hennessy about the multi-tribal war parties raiding the area. Hennessy, a fearless man, refused to listen and departed in spite of Bent's advice. Hennessy and his three teamsters were killed. Their bodies were discovered by Osage buffalo hunters who, in turn, threw the corpses into the teamsters' wagons and burned them. The white people later named the town Hennessey in honor of this man.

The army dispersed four columns of troops to scour the countryside in hot pursuit of the hostile Indians. They relentlessly followed the Cheyenne for months. The troops were so close to the warring Comanches and Cheyenne that the Indians found it almost impossible to resupply during those months. Before summer ended, an additional eight troops of cavalry and four companies of infantry, with artillery, under the command of Colonel Nelson A. Miles, were pursuing the Cheyenne. The hostiles discovered that this white leader tenaciously dogged their every move and maneuver. The army ordered him west following the Civil War, for Miles had already established his reputation as a fierce fighter.

We later learned that this man Miles had been the cruel jailer of Jefferson Davis, the Confederacy's ex-president. At the Civil War's climax, Union forces captured Davis while he was attempting to escape Richmond's fall. Under orders, the 26-year-old Miles imprisoned the Confederate leader at Fort Monroe in Virginia. Miles kept Davis chained to a wall in a cold, dank cell with only a single barred window to allow the light of day to enter. For two years, Davis was subjected to petty tortures. At night, Miles ordered that a light be kept burning in Davis's cell, as two soldiers continuously paced beside his single cot, 24 hours a day. The persistence and wrath of this man now fell upon us.

In 1878, troops under Miles's command would chase 278 half-starved Cheyenne more than 1,500 miles from Oklahoma to Montana. I was one of those. Within 15 years, this former clerk became the U.S. Army's commander in chief and directed the campaigns against all of the West's Indian tribes until they were killed, imprisoned, or put on reservations.

Throughout August of 1874, Miles with his Delaware scouts continued to haunt the very trails the hostile Cheyenne and Comanche followed daily. On the 31st day of that month, he caught up with them at the Washita River's headwaters and engaged them in a running fight. One Cheyenne was killed. To put some distance between themselves and the U.S. Army, the Cheyenne put their trust in a Comanche guide named Mule Smoking. This Comanche guided the Cheyenne through an area unfamiliar to them. He knew all of the water holes in this region known as the Staked Plains. Their good luck to have this guide soon turned to disaster when he became the first casualty in another running fight with Miles's troops. These skirmishes and raids continued for most of summer and early autumn, in present-day Oklahoma and the Texas panhandle.

During this time, Mochi and Medicine Water were still fighting the whites and were holding captive girls by the name of German. I had come down from the north to visit family and again joined the fight when I saw the condition of our people. For two months, Medicine Water and his band avoided capture. His war party and the four white captives suffered many hardships; game was extremely scarce—the buffalo hunters had performed their jobs well. To the Indians, the appearance of Miles's troops seemed to have replaced the buffalo's disappearance throughout the countryside. We were constantly kept on the run. During our flight from the "blue coats," Medicine Water's band sought out Gray Beard's camp on McClellan Creek, east into the Texas panhandle. When we arrived, we found a village of 110 lodges. On the morning of November 8, this camp was discovered by Lieutenant F. D. Baldwin, and he attacked our village without warning. All of our people who were gathered there broke camp abruptly, leaving behind the two youngest German girls. In our departure, I was with the Cheyenne rear guard, who were posted on a hill. We waited there until we saw the girls rescued by the soldiers. The two elder German girls remained with us for two months.

During the month of the Hard-Face Moon (November) of 1874, 10 years after the massacre at Sand Creek, the winter and white soldiers were rapidly approaching the Southern Cheyenne. The harshness of the 1874–75 winter caused Comanche and Kiowa warriors to return to Fort Sill and surrender. Even though we were outnumbered, cold, and hungry, we still refused to submit to white authority. We held out until January 1875, when Agent John Miles sent out friendly Cheyenne runners from Darlington to find us. Their task was to induce us to return to the agency. When the runners found our band, they were shocked at our condition. Our constant running from troops and our attempt to sustain ourselves on little food had taken its toll. Because of the late winter cold and hunger, Agent Miles's messengers convinced most of us to return. Finally, White Horse and Stone Calf agreed to return with the Dog Soldiers. Accompanying Stone Calf's group were the two German girls. The following month, Stone Calf and Red Moon were sent out to contact the remaining hostiles, and in early March, Gray Beard and the majority of the Cheyenne turned themselves in. Among the last to surrender were Medicine Water and his wife, Mochi. The Cheyenne war of 1874–75 was over, but the ordeal of its warriors had just begun.

Having spent two years of his military career as a jailer, Colonel Nelson A. Miles, along with others, decided the most effective way to handle the leaders of this Indian war was to imprison them. Without a trial or tribunal, the leaders of each tribe were arrested, and a decision was made to escort them to the military prison at Fort Marion, Florida. Twenty-six Kiowa, nine Comanche, two Arapaho, and 31 Cheyenne were selected. The army's course of action completely puzzled us Cheyenne. In our custom, any warrior or grown man taken in battle was promptly killed. It was expected and understood as a misfortune of war. To be placed in chains and put into a prison was unacceptable to our beliefs. To us Cheyenne, suicide was not an option either because we had been taught that our spirit would be doomed to walk the earth forever.

Some say Lieutenant Colonel Thomas H. Neill was drunk the day he selected the Cheyenne to be imprisoned. The hard-drinking career officer first chose the leaders, Gray Beard, Heap of Birds (Many Magpies), Eagle Head, Lean Bear (the son of the old chief killed in 1863), Medicine Water, and Mochi. Neill chose Mochi because Sophia German, the youngest surviving girl, accused Mochi of being the person who "chopped my mother's head open with an ax." Hearing this, Neill decided to "cut off

18 from the right of the line." Only the number of Cheyenne, including the chiefs involved, to be sent to prison was important. Many of the 18 were innocent of any wrongdoing, but to Colonel Neill, the point was irrelevant.

The morning of April 6, 1875, was not a routine day for Darlington's blacksmith. The army ordered Wesley, a large, powerful, former slave, to place the 31 prisoners in leg irons. As he started his unpleasant task, he may have remembered his own days of being chained. Whether the memories of those days or the sound of Cheyenne women singing nearby caused him to become uncomfortable, it is unknown. Neither he nor the others present were aware that the women's song was actually taunting the warriors being chained. Their song scorned the warriors with, "Where will we get fathers worth giving sons to? We see there are no men among you worth taking to our beds!" (Sandoz 1953). After having placed several of the Cheyenne into irons, the former slave now confronted a warrior whose battle exploits were near legendary to us. He stood about 5 feet 11 inches and weighed about 185 pounds. Although the muscled warrior was smaller than Wesley, he possessed a massive barrel chest and looks that belied his quickness and agility. His name was Black Horse.[1] He was named in honor of old Chief Black Horse, the man who had helped defeat Fetterman's troops near Fort Phil Kearny nine years earlier. As Wesley attempted to place him in irons, Black Horse kicked him under the chin and ran for his life. Through a hail of the guard's gunfire, Black Horse bolted to open ground beyond the agency's confines. Running as though he were a brother to the prairie wind itself, Black Horse seemed impervious to the bullets flying around him. He felt he could reach the safety of White Horse's camp in the distance. When he was about 30 yards from the camp, Black Horse was knocked to the ground. One of the soldier's bullets had found its mark in Black Horse's side.

He was not alone in his break from the army. Others, including myself, not yet ironed, broke and fled for our freedom. Some of us ran to the fallen Black Horse's aid and dragged him to safety. Well-aimed "indiscriminate" bullets fired through the camp again found innocent victims. Several women and children were wounded by guards trying to "cut down the fleeing Cheyenne prisoners." In a panic, more women and children scurried for the sand hills beyond the Cheyenne camp and began to dig pits in which to escape the slaughter. Other warriors who fled were White Horse and some of his band. His men were poorly armed, but they gathered what rifles and bows and arrows they possessed and dug in for the troops' impending attack. The army, now in force, brought up a Gatling gun for extra firepower.

The younger Cheyenne men moved beyond their camp as the fighting commenced in earnest and dug up the guns they had hidden before the army disarmed them. As the Cheyenne scooped out dirt with their hands to make their position stronger, the wounded Black Horse dragged himself along to the people shouting, "Hold fast!" and "Fight Hard!" Then he sang:

> The women will see they still have men
> To father their sons
> We will not sit in chains!
> It is better to die fighting.
> (Sandoz 1953)

The troops then charged our position in the sand hills, but they were turned back by our entrenchment and accurate shooting. As our resistance intensified the army wheeled forward a Gatling gun and opened fire onto the sand hills. The weapon's barrels spewed its unearthly bullets into our position. Fortunately, the rounds could not penetrate the sand, but its shocking effects terrified many of our women and children who had taken refuge there. Black Horse and other warriors prevented complete panic. Nightfall found us completely surrounded by the army. However, as the troops awaited daylight to finish their job, we used the cover of darkness to slip silently through the surrounding troops, and we vanished into the night. We were later told that the troops were astonished the following day to find that all of us—men, women, and children—had escaped their tightly woven net around the sand hills.

We soon forged our way north to escape the starvation and chains the Indian Territory held for us. Within three days of our Darlington escape, we encountered a group of other Tse Tse Stus who had not yet surrendered. Their leader, Little Bull, had been out all winter. He and his group were on their way to Darlington to surrender. Confronted with the tales of the slaughter occurring at the agency, Little Bull and our group held a brief council. About 20 lodges decided to make a run for it with us, while another faction in camp convinced some of Little Bull's party to return to the agency.

Little Bull, Chicken Hawk, Spotted Wolf, and White Horse decided their safety lay in the north country. They would rather fight to the death than be ironed and caged in a land the whites called Florida. During this time, the army had notified its forts in Kansas to be on the lookout for the fleeing Cheyenne. At Fort Wallace, Kansas, Lieutenant Austin Henely's orders were to head off the Indians and prevent their escape into Nebraska.

After crossing the Smoky Hill River, we again found the army on our trail. We then split into small parties to confuse the pursuing troops. Though we managed to confuse the troops time and again, we could not lose them. Little Bear, Black Horse, and I went with Little Bull's party when he decided to camp on the North Fork of Sappa Creek, in the northwest part of Kansas. This creek was a good place to hide because of its isolated location, and had it not been for blind luck, Lieutenant Henely would never have found us. In the spring of that year, April 1875,

Lieutenant Henely met a group of white buffalo hunters who had seen our camp on Sappa Creek. With thoughts of plundering the village, the hunters agreed to guide Henely and his troops to the creek.

At daybreak on the next day, Henely's troops attacked our camp. As the fighting commenced, his troops rushed across the creek and took positions, where they unleashed a murderous crossfire into our village. The buffalo hunters fired their powerful, long-range rifles so rapidly that it looked as if our people were being executed. Many of their targets were women and children. Little Bull had seen enough. He and Dirty Water finally ventured out to parley with Henely. The lieutenant sent out a sergeant to meet with the two Cheyenne. As the sergeant approached the two men, a warrior named White Bear rose up from his position of cover and fired his rifle. The sergeant died before he knew he had been shot. Without hesitation or an order, the troops opened fire, killing Little Bull and Dirty Water instantly. The sounds of battle again filled the Kansas countryside. The army's firepower and the buffalo hunters' accuracy was so intense that our people were forced to withdraw. Many escaped through this torrent of lead to forge their way north, but White Bear was not one of them. As he rose up to take a final shot at the army and exposed himself to the murderous fire, he was killed. My friend Little Bear, who had survived Sand Creek with me, also died at Sappa Creek. His mother and father had been killed earlier in the fight. In his final act of defiance, he jumped upon his pony and charged into the army's position. The army riddled his body with bullets; only his pony survived the fight. Twenty-seven of our people died that day.

The official U.S. Army reports stated that 19 warriors and eight women and children died on April 23, 1875. But, Shadow, we know for a fact that the only men killed that day were Little Bear, Little Bull, Dirty Water, Tangle Hair, The Rat, White Bear, Young Bear, and Stone Teeth. The other 19 persons killed were women and children.

Black Horse survived the fight at Sappa Creek. He and the rest of us escaped to the north country. Starvation and exposure to the elements punctuated the ordeal we suffered in our 1,500-mile journey in the time we call the Time of the Spring Moon (Matsé'oméeše'he, late May through early June). Black Horse survived to fight another day. He and I counted coup and killed many of our enemies on a June day one year later, the time when the Tse Tse Stus and Lakota (Sioux) met Yellow Hair Custer on the banks of the Little Big Horn River in Montana. We remembered him from eight years before on the Washita River.

The stories of Black Horse's exploits survived the man, who died in 1936. In his lifetime, he fought against the soldiers wherever he found them and raided ranches and farms for years. He eventually settled down here in Lame Deer. He was married three times during his lifetime.

For the 31 Cheyenne prisoners who were ironed and sentenced to Fort Marion, Florida, life changed from their reality to a fantasy world. The Bureau of Indian Affairs ordered Captain Richard Henry Pratt, a young Civil War veteran, to escort the prisoners by train to their Florida destination. Pratt personally felt Indians were people and not savages. This sentiment was unusual among officers in the U.S. Army. His intentions for our people and other Indian prisoners in his custody were positive but somewhat misguided in the direction he took. Pratt thought that if he could take the "Indian out of the man," the man could be salvaged and made into a brown-skinned replica of a White, Anglo-Saxon Protestant. Before implementing his idea, however, his first task was to get his "wards" to prison.

The Indians never forgot their train ride to Florida. For most, it was their first close encounter with the "Iron Horse." The Cheyenne and other prisoners, still in their irons, were put into rail cars. Those irons cut into their flesh so badly that their ankles and wrists were scarred for the rest of their lives. These were scars they never talked about later in life.

The 1,000-mile trip to where the sun "rises from the earth" seemed endless to our people and the other prisoners. Pratt tried to make his presence known to the prisoners a few times a day, not in the role of overlord, but rather as a benevolent caretaker. During one of his tours, Captain Pratt, accompanied by his six-year-old daughter, came in contact with Gray Beard. This Tse Tse Stus chief, speaking through an interpreter, asked the captain in a trembling voice, "How would you like to have chains on your legs, as I have, and be taken a long distance from your home, your wife and little girl, as I have?" (Pratt 1964). Pratt was silent; this was not a question he could easily answer. Gray Beard found his absolution, however, not with the spoken word, but through the smell of gunpowder.

As the train neared the Georgia-Florida state line, one of the guards awoke Pratt and told him a prisoner had escaped. Pratt pulled the emergency cord to stop the train, and as it jarred to a halt, he told the conductor what had happened. During the search, Pratt discovered Gray Beard had freed himself from his chains and jumped from the train through his open window. This Tse Tse Stus warrior had taken his blanket and bundle and had seemingly vanished into the humid southern night. Pratt ordered that the train be backed up, and armed troops soon scoured the Georgia countryside. Then one of the soldiers, a sergeant, spotted Gray Beard's hiding place. He had jumped from the train onto a palmetto tree. As Gray Beard leaped from the tree to escape, the sergeant shouted for him to halt, but Gray Beard spoke no English and probably would not have stopped anyway. The sergeant took aim and shot him in the back. The bullet came out through his chest. Pratt noted, "He was still living. We fixed a place and lifted him into the rear of the last car and brought Manimic [sic], his old friend and war chief and others of his tribe to see him. The interpreter stood by and told me what they said. Among other things Gray Beard said he had wanted to die ever since being chained and taken from home. He told Manimic what to tell his wife and daughter and soon died" (Pratt 1964).

Gray Beard was not the last to die. Upon reaching the old Spanish fort, the Cheyenne knew Death was near, for like Mochi, outside their walls was the Atlantic Ocean, and they too believed it to be the first of the Four Great Rivers. Our blankets and beaded moccasins were traded in for army uniforms. Pratt sought to remove every aspect of our Indian life, including religion, tribal customs, language, and, inadvertently, the natural dignity of the Cheyenne. He wanted to transform our people into the white man's image.

During their three-year prison term, the Cheyenne and others were brought into St. Augustine wearing their uniforms to show the local citizens the progress they were making towards being turned into good white men. The locals purchased the souvenir bows and arrows they made as well as their beadwork. What little money they earned was sent back to the Darlington Agency to help their families. More often than not, their money never reached beyond the pockets of the guards they entrusted it to.

During nonworking and school times, they were allowed to go fishing in the Atlantic Ocean just outside the walls of their prison. They found great excitement in hunting and killing the great Water Buffalo (sharks) that swam through the warm coastal waters. When they committed infractions, they were chained and put into a dark, solitary cell for days or weeks. In one case, Pratt's medical officer sedated an uncooperative Cheyenne prisoner in front of other Indians. They thought the man to be dead. When the drug eventually wore off and this warrior woke up, it convinced the Tse Tse Stus and others that Pratt's "medicine" was so great he could actually resurrect the dead. After this incident he had little trouble with the majority of his inmates.

However, following the first year of their imprisonment, in 1876, we and the Lakota defeated Custer at Little Big Horn, 2,000 miles away. After that shocking news reached St. Augustine's white citizens, the Cheyenne and others confined at the old Spanish fort were no longer allowed their excursions into town.

When Pratt departed Fort Marion in 1879, he took his ideas of transforming Indians into whites with him. Later in 1879, his creation of the Indian Industrial Schools grew from the shell of an old army barracks in Carlisle, Pennsylvania. His first school was aptly named the Carlisle School for the Indians.[2] Pratt's belief that the Indians should be educated into the white man's culture was correct; however, his attempt to destroy our culture in the process was misguided. For many of the Cheyenne who returned to the reservation in Oklahoma after their imprisonment, life was a mixture of their old ways and their new religion and education. Assimilation was very difficult. Few would prosper or rise above the poverty that is still with us. Over the years, alcoholism induced by reservation life has killed more of our people than all the bullets in all our wars. You see, Shadow, many of our people lost their identity and their dignity while white men sought to make us a brown reflection of themselves. Those who did not leave the fort were considered lucky. During their three-year imprisonment, many of the Cheyenne, Kiowa, Arapaho, and Comanche died from the white man's diseases lurking in the depths and darkness of that 300-year-old fort.

We in the north were eventually sent to Oklahoma—what the whites called Indian Territory. But things became so bad there that in 1878, 278 of us left the reservation under the leadership of Dull Knife and Little Wolf. We had almost no ammunition and few horses. Fewer than half of us were adults; the rest were children. For months the U.S. Army pursued us with more than 10,000 troops. Our most valiant warriors died in that terrible time, and it was during this time that I received the wound that makes me limp so badly.

We made it back here to Montana after many of us had perished in that bad winter at Fort Robinson, Nebraska. We had few blankets, and they would give us no firewood to keep us warm. So we burned what we could: old benches and floorboards. There were 130 of us before we broke out of that place. Before the night was over, there were fewer than 100 of us left alive.

This was a terrible time for us, Little One, and I do not wish to remember any more tonight. The indignities our people have suffered extend beyond this life. White scientists have dug up our ancient graves for more than 100 years in the name of research. Can you imagine what would happen to any of our people who attempted to dig up someone in a white man's cemetery? Shortly after the massacre at Sand Creek, the army sent doctors to that terrible place for the sole purpose of digging up our dead and taking them to Washington, D.C., where they were kept in the Smithsonian Institute.[3] It is sad to think about, Shadow, but for those who remember, like myself, I believe that Sweet Medicine's prophecies all came true.

Shadow still remembered the sorrow in the old man's voice when he had spoken those words, and she had implored, "But Nam Shim, do we have to see them all come true? Can't we reverse what has happened?"

Notes

[1]Black Horse's great-grandson is United States Senator Ben Nighthorse Campbell. He is the only Native American serving in Congress, and only the seventh Native American in history to hold office in either house.

[2]Carlisle's most famous student was Jim Thorpe, considered to be one of the greatest athletes of all time. Thorpe came from the Sac-Fox nations in Oklahoma to Carlisle about 1905.

[3]Since 1993, the Cheyenne and other tribes have forced the Smithsonian Institute and other museums, through legal action, to return the bodies and body parts for tribal burials.

References

Pratt, Richard Henry. 1964. *Battlefield and Classroom: Four Decades with the American Indian, 1867–1904.* Hartford, CT: Yale University Press.

Sandoz, Mari. 1953. *Cheyenne Autumn.* New York: McIntosh & Otis.

Discussion and Activities

Goal

■ Recount the last year of freedom for the Cheyenne and Arapaho before they were sent to prison or reservations.

Discussion Questions

1. What started the last of the Southern Cheyenne wars in 1874?

   Answer: The slaughter of the buffalo herds by the whites.

2. In which state was the battle at Adobe Walls fought?

   Answer: Texas, in the panhandle.

3. Who built the Adobe Walls fort?

   Answer: William Bent, in the 1840s.

4. Black Horse was a famous Cheyenne warrior. Who is his now-famous great-grandson?

   Answer: United States Senator Ben Nighthorse Campbell.

5. Isatai was the Comanche medicine man who planned the failed attack on Adobe Walls. What does his name translate into in English?

   Answer: Rear-End-of-a-Wolf.

6. Who was the woman warrior who survived the massacre at Sand Creek and later held captive young girls from the German family?

   Answer: Mochi, also called Buffalo Calf Woman.

7. Who was her husband?

   Answer: Medicine Water.

8. After the final surrender of the Southern Cheyenne, how many were selected to go to prison?

   Answer: 31. Among the prisoners were Mochi and Medicine Water. Mochi was the only known Native American female prisoner of war. She was taken to Fort Marion prison in St. Augustine, Florida.

9. Where did Black Horse go when he made his escape from being chained and ironed?

   Answer: He made an unbelievable 1,500-mile journey, after being wounded, from Oklahoma to Montana, where he participated in the Battle of Little Big Horn a year later.

10. Why did the idea of imprisonment puzzle the Cheyenne warriors?

    Answer: According to their customs, any warrior taken in a battle was killed. It was expected. Being placed in chains and imprisoned was unacceptable.

Things to Do

Writing Activity

Building on the information that students have acquired from the stories in this book, have them work with partners and brainstorm everything they remember about the Cheyenne culture and history. Have each student choose one story or event that they think is important and write a short paragraph recounting the story or event and why they chose it. Have students share what they have written with the class.

Discussion Activity

The stories and events recounted in this book are told from the Cheyenne point of view. With the students, discuss historical point of view and how the accounts of historical events are different, depending on the perspective from which they are told. Lead a class discussion about the history of the white man's movement across the continental United States, first from the viewpoint of the Native Americans, then from the viewpoint of the white man. Use this opportunity to help students examine historical accounts critically to understand both sides of the event.

Class Bulletin Board

With students, construct a timeline of the events narrated in chapters six through nine. Place the timeline on the class bulletin board. Connect these events with the geographic areas on the map. (This can be done with yarn or string.) In this way, students will gain an understanding not only of the sequence of events, but of the vast area in which they took place.

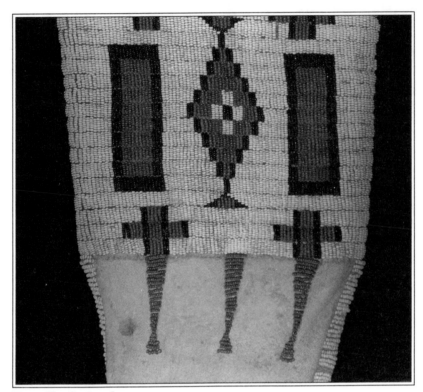

Detail of pipe bag

10

There Are No Good-byes

The old man was silent for a long time, then he told Shadow, "Little One, no one can reverse what has already happened, but we can learn from these stories of our culture. What I have been doing is giving you these stories with the hope that you will never forget them. And, that one day you will tell them to others exactly as I have told them to you. In this way you will keep our culture and language alive to those who would hear you. Never be ashamed of who you are or what you believe. Shadow, you are Tse Tse Stus, just like Mochi, who was a great warrior. Our language and culture must never die. This is all I will ever ask of you. Live your life in a good way. Judge no one by their religion or color, only by their deeds. And always keep our ancient campfires warm with our stories."

Shadow never forgot these words. They were as fresh and clear in her mind at that moment as the first time she heard them. It was now time for her final journey with Old Nam Shim to end. They had arrived at the large cottonwood tree where she and Nam Shim's grandson had constructed the scaffold. Gently and reverently they hoisted his body up to the scaffold, using the pulleys they'd set up for this task. Then they secured his body in place. There were more prayers and a few final tears, but there would be no good-byes. It was Nam Shim who had taught her to speak in the ancient tongue of the Tse Tse Stus. He told her that there was no word for good-bye in their language. There was only "Until I see you again" (Nėstaévåhósevóomåtse).

This is what she said as she turned to leave. Slowly, she and Nam Shim's grandson headed back towards their home. They had been gone for most of the day, and the sun was starting to set. As they passed along the banks of the Tongue River, something caught Shadow's eye—the sunlight on the river. As she watched the "water spirits" light their torches for the night, she also saw something else. It was the figure of an old man sitting by the river. Slowly he stood up and looked toward Shadow. It was Old Nam Shim. Before he started his journey across the Four Great Rivers, he had stopped by this river that had meant so much to him in life. He had come back to tell Shadow, "Everything is all right."

He smiled at Shadow, and she didn't turn away from his spirit. She smiled, too, and said, as he slowly vanished, "Until I see you again," Nam Shim. "Until I see you again." And then, as if almost in a tearful whisper, Shadow said, "There are no good-byes."

Vocabulary

English Words

The following words that may be unfamiliar to students were used in this book. This list provides a definition for these words.

affidavit	Written declaration under oath.
ambush	The act of lying in wait to attack by surprise.
atone	To make amends for something done wrong.
atrocity	An act of extreme cruelty.
awl	A pointed tool for making holes, as in leather or wood.
benevolent	Something or someone good.
cactus	Any variety of a leafless, fleshy-stemmed, often spiny plant.
carnage	Massive slaughter, as in war.
ceremonial	An object or person characterized by a ceremony.
ceremonial pipe	A pipe; its bowl is made of red pipe stone and a long stem made of wood. Used for prayer.
Conquistador	A soldier from Spain who helped conquer Mexico and Peru.
counting coup	The act of striking an enemy with a stick without killing him.
creator	The name given to God by Cheyenne and other Plains people.
crier	One who shouts out public announcements.
defiance	An act of resistance to authority.
defy	To resist.
deity	A god.
delegation	A group of people authorized to represent others.
depredation	An act of destruction or plunder or savagery.
dry meat (a kind of jerky)	Meat cut off of an animal and hung to preserve it for eating later.
duel	A prearranged fight between two persons.
embrace	To take up willingly.
eulogize	To deliver a speech of praise for someone.
exploits	Notable acts or deeds; a heroic feat.
impulse	A motivating force or spontaneous inclination.
insulated	To detach or isolate.

interpreter	A person who is a translator.
Lakota	The name of a Native American people commonly called Sioux.
lamentation	To express great sorrow.
lariat	A rope with a running noose.
lore	Tradition or belief about a specific subject.
lodge	A circular dwelling made of animal skins; commonly called "tipi."
midwife	A woman who assists women during childbirth.
mourn	To grieve; to feel sorrow.
parfleche	Split buffalo rawhide that is used to make pouches or containers, normally painted in traditional colors and used for storage in lodges or on horses.
Pawnee	An aggressive Plains people—traditional enemy of Tse Tse Stus and Lakota.
pemmican	Mixture of dry meat, berries, and fat (used like trail mix is used today).
placenta	A membrane that joins the unborn child and mother during pregnancy. The unborn child is attached to the placenta by the umbilical cord. The placenta acts as a filter system.
prairie	An extensive area of flat or rolling grassland.
prediction	To make something known in advance.
prophet	One who speaks by divine inspiration or a prediction.
prophecy	A prediction; an inspired utterance of a prophet.
prosperous	Having success; flourishing.
Purgatory	A place where souls go after death to atone for sins.
quarrel	A dispute or argument.
quill (v.)	The process of using porcupine quills for decoration. The quills were soaked in hot animal fat, flattened by biting them, and then woven into colorful designs.
reality	The condition or quality of being real or true.
reminisce	Recalling a past experience.
revenge	To inflict punishment in return for injury or insult.
reverent/irreverent	Feeling profound respect for someone or something.
riding crop	A small whip, normally made of buffalo tail and horse hair.
scaffold	Used in Native American funerals; made of four branches and animal skins. The dead are placed in this after it has been fastened to a tree or four poles.
stallion	A male horse.
stockade	Small fort-like structure normally made of logs.

sustain	To keep in existence.
sweat (n.)	The process of going into a hot, steaming lodge to purify the body and the soul.
tenacious	Holding firmly or stubborn.
thunderbird	Mythical creature of Tse Tse Stus (Tsétsehéstahese) and other Plains people; its wings create terrible windstorms, and its claws cause lightning and thunder.
yearlings	An animal that is a year old.
universe	The earth, all living things, and all the stars and planets.
vigilante	An unauthorized group (or individual) that takes on itself the powers of pursuing and punishing those suspected of being criminals.
wash (n.)	A small ravine (mini-canyon).

Cheyenne Words

Because the Cheyenne language was originally only a spoken language, there is still disagreement about the spelling of words. In this book we use more than one spelling of a number of words in recognition of these differing opinions.

Guide to Pronunciations

Cheyenne vowels include a, e, and o.

—Usually *e* sounds like a short *i* in English, such as in the word *mitten*.

—Usually *o* sounds like a long o in English, such as in the word *wrote*.

—When found at the end of a single word or at the end of a phrase, Cheyenne vowels are whispered. When a whispered vowel is found within a word, it is denoted with a small circle above the vowel. For example: e̊.

—Pitch: ' indicates a high pitch. ~ indicates a middle pitch. ´ indicates a low tone or pitch. A difference in pitch may indicate an entirely different word, so it is very important.

Cheyenne consonants include h, k, m, n, p, s, t, v, x, and '.

'—glottal stop. A quick stop in a vowel sound, not found in the English language. This sound can be heard in the phrase "uh-oh."

x—the Cheyenne letter *x* resembles a common sound in the German language as the "ch" sound in their word *Achtung!*

š—the Cheyenne letter *s* is pronounced "esh."

Sources

Leman, Wayne, and Ted Risingsun. 1990. *Let's Talk Cheyenne: An Audio Cassette Course.* Busby, CCEP.

Leman, Wayne, and Josephine Stands In Timber Glenmore. 1986. *Cheyenne Topical Dictionary.* Busby, Cheyenne Translation Project.

Cheyenne spellings used in book	Cheyenne pronunciations	English translations
His Stah	Hésta'he	Belly Button
Hupéneohótuah'e	Hupéneohótuah'e	Buffalo Medicine Man
Maheo	Ma'heõ'o	sacred power/god
Ma Guss	Ma'kõ'se	The Youngest
Mehn	Mé hne	water serpent
Mochi	Mo ke, or Mó'kė̊huduovse	Buffalo Calf Woman
Nam Shim	Namė̊šéme	grandfather
Seyon	Seyon	Place of the Dead
Tse Tse Stus	Tsétsė̊héstahese	Our People (Cheyenne)
ve hoe	vé'ho'e	white man

Cheyenne pronunciations	English translations
Ahtó nové'ho'e	The Wise One Below
ésevone	buffalo
éškỏseome	lodge
He'ámávé'ho'e	The Wise One Above
Heévåhetaneo'o	Hair Rope Men
He'konéneéše'he	November (literally, Time of the Hard-Face Moon)
Heóve'hó'nehe	Yellow Wolf
Hohtséeše'he	January (literally, Time of the Hoop Moon)
ka'ėškóne	child
ka'ėškoneho	children
ma'aetaemèò'o	White man's train (literally, iron horse)
Matsé'oméeše'he	May (literally, Time of the Spring Moon)
Mó'ỏhtávetoo'o	Black Kettle
nåháa'e	aunt
náhko'e	mother
na'šhivatúmnátutse	my poor pets
ného'e	father
néške'e	grandmother
Nėstaévåhósevóomåtse	Until I see you again (a Cheyenne parting)
Nóvávóse	Bear Butte (literally, giving hill), The Sacred Mountain
Póénẽõ ó'he'e	Sand Creek (literally, Dry Creek)
séoto	ghost/spirit
Vé'ho'kẽso	Little White Man
vo'ėstane	person

Additional Cheyenne Words and Sayings

Note: Many of the terms listed here were not used in this book, *Four Great Rivers to Cross*. They have been added to enrich further studies of some Tse Tse Stus words.

Above	he'ama
Big Dipper	ma'xetoeneš ko
Bread	kóhkonȯheo'o
Brother	nȧhtatáméme
Cow	vé'ho'éotóá'a
Deer	váótséva
Don't do that	Néve'nȅhešéve!
Go to sleep	Tanaóotsȅstse!
Good day (It is a good day)	Epahavatamano e
He is crazy	émȧsȅhánee'e
He is brave	éháahe
Horse	mo'éhno'ha
I love you	nȅméhuotatsé
It is cold	Etonéto
It is windy	éháá'ha
Milky Way	Améó'o
Rain	hoo'kȯho
Sister	hemeho
Sit down	Hámȅstoo'ȅstse
Snake	šé'šenovoto
Snow	hésta'se
Spider	vé'ho'e (this word is also used for "White man")
Star	hotȯhke
Sun	éšhe'he
Sugar	vé'keemahpe
Teacher	vovestomósanéhe
Thank you	hahoo (for men); néá'eše (for women)
Uncle	Ného'e (same word used for father)
Water	mahpe

Recommended Additional Reading

Berthrong, Donald J. 1963. *The Southern Cheyenne*. Norman: University of Oklahoma Press.

    This book contains a good overview of the history of the Cheyenne. The author is still alive.

Brown, Dee. 1970. *Bury My Heart at Wounded Knee*. New York: Holt, Rinehart & Winston.

    This book chronicles the history of Native Americans from their meeting with Columbus to the slaughter of Lakota people in Wounded Knee, SD, in 1890.

———. 1984. *The Fetterman Massacre*. Lincoln: University of Nebraska Press.

    This books details the incident at Fort Phil Kearny in 1866.

Grinnell, George Bird. 1962. *The Cheyenne Indians*. Lanham, MD: Cooper Square.

    Grinnell lived with the Cheyenne shortly after the wars and wrote during the last nineteenth century. This book, originally published in the early twentieth century, details the history of the Cheyenne in the nineteenth century. George Bent was his chief resource and interpreter.

Hoig, Stan. 1961. *The Sand Creek Massacre*. Norman: University of Oklahoma Press.

    This definitive study of the massacre at Sand Creek contains some errors.

Hyde, George. *The Life of George Bent, Written from His Letters*. Norman: University of Oklahoma Press.

    This is the only written account of the Native American side of the story of the mid- to late-nineteenth century events.

Magoffin, Susan. 1926. *Down the Santa Fe Trail and into Mexico: The Diary of Susan Magoffin, 1846–1847*. Lincoln: University of Nebraska Press.

    This book explains what life was like for white people traveling and settling along the Santa Fe Trail.

Mendoza, Patrick M. 1993. *Song of Sorrow: Massacre at Sand Creek*. Denver, CO: Willow Wind.

    This is a narrative version of the massacre at Sand Creek that contains family stories and information never before published.

Sandoz, Mari. 1953. *Cheyenne Autumn*. New York: MacIntosh and Otis.

    This book chronicles the odyssey of the Cheyenne's journey from Oklahoma back to Montana in 1878.

References

Ambrose, Stephen E. 1975. *Crazy Horse and Custer: The Parallel Lives of Two American Warriors*. College Park, MD: Meridian.

Ashley, Susan Riley. 1936. Reminiscences of Colorado in the Early Sixties. *The Colorado Magazine* xiii: 219–30.

Bent, Lucille (granddaughter of George Bent). 1990 through 1994. Interviews by author in Clinton, OK.

Berthrong, Donald J. 1963. *The Southern Cheyenne*. Norman: University of Oklahoma Press.

———. 1976. *The Cheyenne and Arapaho Ordeal*. Norman: University of Oklahoma Press.

———. 1989. Interview by author in West Lafayette, IN.

Big Medicine, Joe (Ceremonial Priest to Keeper of Sacred Medicine Arrows). 1991, 1992, 1997. Interviews by author in Longdale, OK.

Brown, Dee. 1970. *Bury My Heart at Wounded Knee*. New York: Holt, Rinehart & Winston.

———. 1984. *The Fetterman Massacre*. Lincoln: University of Nebraska Press. Formerly titled *Fort Phil Kearny, an American Saga*. 1962. New York: Putnam.

Bull, Richard Tall (a chief of the Northern Cheyenne), an oral historian. 1989. Interview by author in Denver, CO.

Campbell, U.S. Senator Ben Nighthorse (a chief of the Northern Cheyenne). 1989, 1990, 1991. Interviews by author in Pueblo and Durango, CO, and Washington, DC.

Capps, Benjamin. 1973. *The Old West: The Indians*. Alexandria, VA: Time-Life Books.

Cardinal, Jack (Mat'O, Shoshoni storyteller). 1989, 1990, 1991. Interview by author in Thornton, CO.

Carrington, Margaret Irvin. 1983. *Absaraka: Home of the Crows*. Philadelphia, PA: J. B. Lippincott.

Craig, Reyinald S. 1959. *The Fighting Parson*. Tucson, AZ: Westernlore Press.

Davis, Burke. 1985. *The Long Surrender*. New York: Random House.

Goose, Sherman (Southern Cheyenne elder). 1993, 1994, 1995, 1996, 1997. Interviews by author in Arapaho, OK.

Grinnell, George B. 1915. *The Fighting Cheyennes.* Norman: University of Oklahoma Press.

———. 1962. *The Cheyenne Indians.* Lanham, MD: Cooper Square.

Hall, Frank. 1896. *History of Colorado. 1889-1895.*

Hanway, Paul (Northern Arapaho). 1989, 1990, 1991. Interviews by author in Denver, CO.

Hoig, George E. 1961. *The Sand Creek Massacre.* Norman: University of Oklahoma Press.

Hyde, George. 1937. *Red Cloud's Folk: A History of the Oglala Sioux Indians.* Norman: University of Oklahoma Press.

Joint Committee on the Conduct of the War, Massacre of the Cheyenne Indians, 38th Congress, Second Session. 1865. *The Sand Creek Massacre: A Documentary History.* Washington DC. Report of the Secretary of War, 39th Congress, Second Session. Senate Executive Document no. 26, Washington DC, 1867. New York: Sol Lewis Publisher, 1973.

Lavender, David. 1954. *Bent's Fort.* Lincoln: University of Nebraska Press.

Leonard, Stephen J., and Thomas J. Noel. 1990. *Denver: Mining Camp to Metropolis.* Boulder: University Press of Colorado.

Magoffin, Susan. 1926. *Down the Santa Fe Trail and into Mexico: The Diary of Susan Magoffin, 1846–1847.* Lincoln: University of Nebraska Press.

Mendoza, Patrick M. 1993. *Song of Sorrow: Massacre at Sand Creek.* Denver, CO: Willow Wind.

Noel, Thomas J. 1982. *The City and the Saloon.* Lincoln: University of Nebraska Press.

Panana, Marcella (great-great-great-granddaughter of Yellow Wolf). 1990, 1991, 1995, 1996, 1997. Interviews by author in Clinton, OK.

Peterson, Dale. 1982. *A Mad People's History of Madness.* Pittsburgh, PA: University of Pittsburgh Press.

Pratt, Richard Henry. 1964. *Battlefield and Classroom: Four Decades with the American Indian, 1867–1904.* Lincoln: University of Nebraska Press.

Prairie, Robert Chief (Southern Cheyenne). 1990, 1991. Interviews by author in Clinton, OK.

Sandoz, Mari. 1953. *Cheyenne Autumn.* New York: McIntosh and Otis.

Sawyer, Tom Hayden (great-great-grandson of John Evans). 1989, 1990, 1991. Interviews by author in Evergreen, CO.

Sipes, Mrs. Cleo (great granddaughter of Medicine Water and Mochi [Buffalo Calf Woman]). 1992 through 1997. Interviews by author in Clinton, OK.

Sipes, John L. (great-great-grandson of Medicine Water and Mochi [Buffalo Calf Woman]; Southern Cheyenne Tribal historian for the Oklahoma Historic Society). 1992 through 1997. Interviews by author in Clinton, OK.

Soule, Silas. December 18, 1864, and January 8, 1865. Two letters to his mother.

Stern, Thomas D. 1979. The Controversial Career of Edward W. Wynkoop. *The Colorado Magazine*, 56 (1,2).

Strange Owl, Ann (great-great-granddaughter of William Bent and Owl Woman). 1989, 1990, 1991, 1993, 1994, 1996, 1997. Interviews by author in Loveland, CO.

Trenholm, Virginia Cole (lived and worked with the Arapaho and Shoshonis for 50 years). 1990, 1991. Interviews by author in Cheyenne, WY.

Utley, Robert M. 1988. *Cavalier in Buckskin*. Norman: University of Oklahoma Press.

Wilson, Bertha (granddaughter of woman who survived Washita slaughter in 1868). 1991, 1995, 1996. Interviews by author in Clinton, OK.

Wilson, Elinor. 1914. *Jim Beckwourth: Black Mountain Man, War Chief of the Crows*. Norman: University of Oklahoma Press.

Wilson, Terry (great grandson of Mochi and Medicine Water; Ceremonial Priest to Keeper of the Sacred Medicine Arrows). 1989 through 1997. Interviews by author.

Wynkoop, Edward W. Unfinished manuscript, Colorado History MSS II-20. Denver: Colorado State Historical Society, 28.

Index

About the Authors

Patrick Mendoza is an internationally known storyteller, author, singer, composer, humorist, musician, and photographer who has appeared throughout the United States, Canada, and the British Isles since 1976. His work has been heard on National Public Radio numerous times and his repertoire of original musical productions, songs, and stories has earned him an audience comprised of all age groups.

Pat's first storytelling nonfiction book, *Song of Sorrow: Massacre at Sand Creek* is now in its third printing and is used in history and anthropology classes in junior and senior high schools, colleges, and universities throughout the United States and is under option for a screen play adaptation with a Hollywood producer. In January 1997, Pat was a consultant for a PBS special on the Sand Creek Massacre that aired in January and April (*Tears in the Sand*, Rocky Mountain Legacy).

Pat, a formally adopted Cheyenne, is a Vietnam veteran and has been a policeman, bounty hunter, professional diver, power lifter, and martial arts instructor (he holds black belts in two different styles of karate), and he has recorded numerous storytelling tapes and two musical CDs.

Mendoza is available to visit schools and businesses. Contact him at (303) 388-8097.

Ann Strange Owl-Raben was raised in the small village of Birney, Montana, on the Northern Cheyenne reservation. Her Cheyenne name is Måxaáéhma'héone (Medicine Eagle Feather Woman). Ann left her reservation to work with the Indian Health Service and has since traveled the United States exhibiting her beadwork, acted as an advisor to numerous museums, and current owns and operates Eagle Plume's, a historic Indian trading post in the Colorado high country, with her husband, Dayton Raben, and their daughter, Nico.

Photograph by Lee Milne

About the Authors

Nico Strange Owl, whose Cheyenne name is Esevonemé'ėhné'e (Buffalo Appearing Woman), was raised in both the Cheyenne and mainstream American cultures and strives to educate others about her heritage in order to promote greater understanding. Nico attended Colorado State University from 1981 to 1986 where she studied anthropology. She has since managed three art galleries that featured Indian art, lectured on the subject of Indian art, acted as an advisor to museums, and organized powwows. She also works as an appraiser of Indian art and antiquities.

Photograph by Lee Milne

From **Teacher Ideas Press**

GALLOPING ALONG THE OLD WEST TRAILS: An Integrated Social Studies Unit
Gary M. Garfield and Suzanne McDonough

Take students on a cowboy's journey from St. Louis to the Pacific through letters he writes to and receives from the Old West characters he meets along the way. With art projects, journal writing, newspaper reporting, cooking, gardening, math, computer simulation, science, and many more hands-on activities, students get an authentic picture of pioneer life in the Old West. (Letters are in print and on disk for your convenience!) **Grades 4–8**.
xxii, 183p. 8½x11 paper ISBN 1-56308-475-9

THE PERSONA BOOK: Curriculum-Based Enrichment for Educators
Katherine Grimes Lallier and Nancy Robinson Marino

Watch as your students "become" historical figures of the past! Students choose a literary or historical figure, participate in events as that person, and create projects based on the character's life. This book describes the concept of persona-based enrichment and offers five complete units. **Grades 4–7**.
x, 193p. 8½x11 paper ISBN 1-56308-443-0

EXPLORING DIVERSITY: Literature Themes and Activities for Grades 4–8
Jean E. Brown and Elaine C. Stephens

Take the riches of multicultural literature beyond the printed page and into the classroom. With a variety of themes, discussion questions, and activities that challenge misconceptions and stereotypes, this book gives students the opportunity to develop an understanding of and appreciation for their own and other cultures. **Grades 4–8**.
x, 210p. 8½x11 paper ISBN 1-56308-322-1

AMAZING AMERICAN WOMEN: 40 Fascinating 5-Minute Reads
Kendall Haven

These concise, action-packed reads detail the stories of some of the women who helped shape our nation. The stories are so enlightening and inspiring that some students have been known to read more about these heroes ON THEIR OWN! A great springboard for study across the curriculum. **All Levels**.
xxii, 305p. paper ISBN 1-56308-291-8

LIVES OF PROMISE: Studies in Biography and Family History
Jerry D. Flack

Building on young people's natural curiosity about others, Flack guides students through the steps of researching and writing a biography or autobiography, offering a diversity of delightful, educational activities that invite youngsters to explore their history with tools such as maps, photo albums, and address books. **All Levels**.
Gifted Treasury Series; Jerry D. Flack, Ed.
x, 177p. 8½x11 paper ISBN 1-56308-045-1

For a FREE catalog or to place an order, please contact:

Teacher Ideas Press
Dept. B51 · P.O. Box 6633 · Englewood, CO 80155-6633
1-800-237-6124, ext. 1 · Fax: 303-220-8843 · E-mail: lu-books@lu.com

 Check out the TIP Web site!
www.lu.com/tip